Geography Matters

FOUNDATION

Series Editor:

John Hopkin

Editor:

Paul Brooker

Authors:

Nicola Arber with Jill Sim and Rachel McCarthy, Bournville School, Birmingham

Sue Lomas, Henbury High School, Macclesfield

Garrett Nagle, St Edward's School, Oxford

Linda Thompson, formerly at Sandbach School, Sandbach

Paul Thompson, Ounsdale High School, Wolverhampton

Heinemann

Heinemann Educational Publishers
Halley Court, Jordan Hill, Oxford, OX2 8EJ
a division of Reed Educational & Professional Publishing Ltd
Heinemann is a registered trademark of Reed Educational & Professional Publishing Ltd

OXFORD MELBOURNE AUCKLAND
JOHANNESBURG BLANTYRE GABORONE
IBADAN PORTSMOUTH NH (USA) CHICAGO

First published 2001

ISBN 0 435 35506 6

05 04 03 02 01
10 9 8 7 6 5 4 3 2 1

Designed and illustrated by Gecko Ltd, Bicester, Oxon, Dave Mostyn and Peter Bull
Original illustrations © Heinemann Educational Publishers 2000
Printed and bound in the UK by Bath Colour Books

Acknowledgements
The authors and publishers would like to thank the following for permission to use copyright material:

Maps and extracts
p.6, 7 Philips Foundation Atlas 7th Edition / George Philip Ltd; **p.13** Maps reproduced from Ordnance Survey maps with the permission of the Controller of Her Majesty's Stationary Office © Crown Copyright; License No. 398020; **p.14, 16** McDonald's; **p.26** Encarta / Microsoft Corporation; **p.30** Key Geography Interactions / Stanley Thornes; **p.30** Kandilli Observatory, Istanbul; **p.33** Angela Topping, After the Earthquake, first published in Can Your Hear? Poems / Oxfam, Pan Macmillan 1992. Reproduced by permission of Oxfam GB; **p.34** National Earthquake Information Centre; **p.37** Earthquake Engineering Research Institute; **p.41** SITREP 16, 13th March 2000 / UNICEF; **p.51** UK Census Bureau; **p.56** Philips Foundation Atlas 7th Edition / George Philip Ltd; **p.62, 63, 64, 65, 66** Maps reproduced from Ordnance Survey maps with the permission of the Controller of Her Majesty's Stationary Office © Crown Copyright; License No. 398020; **p.79** The Sunday Telegraph, 1st November 1998; **p.83** Easter 1998 Flood report, Volume 1 / Environmental Agency; **p.84, 86** www.guardianunlimited.co.uk / The Guardian; **p.85** The Guardian 4th March, 10th March 2000, 28th March 2000; **p.86** The Daily Telegraph 29th March 2000; **p.94** Philips Foundation Atlas 7th Edition / George Philip Ltd; **p.96** The Met Office; **p.101, 106** The Football Association Premier League National Fan Survey 1998/99; **p.105** London Transport Museum; **p.105** Chiltern Railways; **p.108, 111, 112** Maps reproduced from Ordnance Survey maps with the permission of the Controller of Her Majesty's Stationary Office © Crown Copyright; License No. 398020; **p.109** Aston Local Plan / Department of Planning, Birmingham City Council; **p.114** Philips Foundation Atlas 7th Edition / George Philip Ltd.

Photographs
Cover photos by Tony Stone and PA News.
4 A Corbis /Craig Aurness; **4 B** Corbis / Yann Arthus-Bertrand; **4 C** Corbis / Catherine Karnow; **4 D** Gettyone Stone; **4 E** Corbis / Galen Rowell; **4 F** The Stock Market; **5 G** Corbis / Paul A.Souders; **5 H** Corbis / Vince Streano; **6** SPL/ NRSC Ltd; **8 A** SPL/Tom Van Sant/ Geosphere Project/ Planetary Visions; **10 A** Dave Marriott – Wimpy; **14 F** Corbis / Owen Franken; **20 A** Associated Press; **20 B** Corbis / AFP; **20 C** Corbis / Nik Wheeler; **20 D** Associated Press; **20 E** Corbis / AFP; **21 F;** Associated Press; **21 G** Corbis / George Hall; **21 H** Associated Press; **21 I** Rex Features / Sipa Press; **21 J** Rex Features / Sipa Press; **25 A** GeoScience Features Picture Library; **27 C** Corbis / Bettmann; **27 D** Rex Features / Sipa Press; **28 F** Rex Features / Sipa Press; **28 G** Corbis / Yann Arthus-Bertrand; **28 H** Rex Features / Sipa Press; **28 K** Rex Features / Sipa Press; **29 L** Tokai University Research & Information Center (TRIC); **29 M** Corbis /Paul A. Souders; **32 A** Rex Features / Sipa Press; **32 B** Rex Features / Sipa Press; **32 E** Associated Press; **32 F** Associated Press; **32 D** Corbis / AFP; **32 C** Corbis / Joseph Sohm; **33** Rex Features / Sipa Press; **34 D** Rex Features / Sipa Press; **35 E** Rex Features / Sipa Press; **36 K** Corbis / AFP; **36 J** Rex Features / Sipa Press; **38 A** Corbis / Craig Lovell; **38 B** Earthquake Hazard Centre / Rajendra Desai; **38 C** Camera Press; **39 E** SPL/David Parker; **39 F** SPL/David Parker; **37 N** Corbis / AFP; **40 B** U.S. Agency for International Development and the Miami-Dade Fire Rescue Squad; **42 A** SPL; **42 B** James Davis Worldwide; **42 C** Corbis / Michael S. Yamashita; **44 A** Corbis / John Noble; **47 C** Eye Ubiquitous; **48 D** Gettyone Stone; **49 E** Corbis / Wolfgang Kaehler; **50 A** The Stock Market; **52 A** The Stock Market; **55 C** Panos Pictures; **55 D** Panos Pictures; **56 B** Corbis / Morton Beebe; **56 C** Still Pictures; **57 D** Gettyone Stone; **57 E** The Stock Market; **58 A** Corbis / Charles & Josette Lenars; **58 B** Corbis / Paul A. Souders; **58 C** Corbis / Uwe Walz; **59 E** Gettyone Stone; **59 D** SPL/Rosenfled Images Ltd; **59 F** Panos Pictures; **59 G** John Hopkin; **62 B** Photoair; **62 D** Britain on View; **63 F** Photoair; **64 G** Welsh Tourist Board; **65 J** Welsh Tourist Board; **66** Worcester Tourist board; **69 A** Sue Cunningham / SCP; **70 C** Corbis; **70 D** Sue Cunningham / SCP; **71 E** Sue Cunningham; **72 F** Sue Cunningham; **72 G** Environmental Images; **74 A** Press Association; **75 B** Newsteam International; **78 A** Alan Bowring; **79 B** Press Association; **82 A** Coventry Evening Standard; **85 A** Associated Press / Karel Prinsloo Stringer; **85 B** Associated Press / Karel Prinsloo Stringer; **86 C** Associated Press / Juda Ngwenya; **86 D** Press Association; **88 B** Britain on View; **88 C** Gettyone Stone; **88 D** Britain on View; **89 D** Bubbles; **89 A** Gettyone Stone; **92 H** Gettyone Stone; **92 A** The Stock Market; **92 B** Gettyone Stone; **92 C** Gettyone Stone; **92 I** The Stock Market; **92 D** Britain on View; **92 E** The Stock Market; **92 F** Tony Stone; **92 G** Bluewater; **93 A** Tony Stone; **93 C** John Hopkin; **93 B** John Hopkin; **93 D** John Hopkin; **93 E** John Hopkin; **97 C** University of Dundee; **100 A** Gettyone Stone; **100 B** Garrett Nagle; **100 C** The Stock Market; **100 D** Panos Pictures / Jeremy Horner; **103 D** Popperfoto; **106 C** Corbis / TempSport; **109 C** Skyscan; **110 F** John Hopkin; **111 B** Garrett Nagle; **112 D** Garrett Nagle.

Contents

Throughout the book these symbols are used with activities that use literacy, numeracy and ICT skills.

A An oasis in the Sahara desert, near Timbuktu

B The River Amazon

Learn about

In this unit you will learn about the connections between places in different parts of the world and how they are connected to places you know.

You will also find out how to carry out an enquiry. This is the way that geographers find out more about things they want to know. You will learn:

- how to locate places on atlas maps
- how to ask geographical questions
- how to collect and present data
- how to make conclusions.

C Bombay

D New York

E The North Pole

F St Lucia

G Sydney

H Mount Fuji, Japan

Activities

1 a Choose one of the photos **B–H**. Think of three questions that you would like to ask about the place, and write them down. Here are some ideas for photo **A**:

- 🌀 Why are there so few plants there?
- 🌀 Does anyone live in that place?
- 🌀 What animals would you find there?
- 🌀 What country is it?

b Compare your questions with those of a partner. Choose the three questions that you think are the most interesting and see if you can find some answers. Use an atlas, library books, CD-ROMs or the Internet to gather your information. **ICT**

c Draw an **annotated** sketch of your chosen photo, like the one in **I** below. Add all the information that you have found out.

How to ...

... draw an annotated sketch

🌀 A sketch that is *annotated* has labels describing its main features. Sometimes these labels will explain a feature too.

The sky is blue with very little cloud, so the weather is very hot during the day.

There is little rainfall in this area so most of the ground is bare.

Animals are adapted to the hot, dry **climate**, like the camel which has a hump to store fat.

People's clothes are light in colour to reflect the heat and to keep them cool.

Trees grow where there is a water supply, for example at an oasis

I An annotated sketch of an oasis

Activities

3 With your partner, look at photos **A–H**. Put the photos into pairs by making connections between them. For example, you can see that photos **A** and **B** both have trees. There might be more than one correct answer, and some that you cannot see. Here are some clues, but see if you can find some unusual connections for yourself:

Pair	Connection
A and B	Both have trees
	both have a dry climate
	both are in Asia
	both are English speaking places

Where in the world?

All the places in the photos on pages 4 and 5 can be found using an **atlas**. An atlas is a book of maps which shows different physical and human features of the world.

The *contents page* of an atlas is found at the front. It contains lists of different countries or continents. You can see a typical contents page in **A**.

The *index* at the back of the atlas will help you find a particular place. Places are listed in alphabetical order. The entry will give the page number and a grid square reference, and the latitude and longitude may also appear. The index entry for Manchester is shown in **B**. Map **D** shows the area around Manchester on an atlas map.

A

BRITISH ISLES SECTION

2–3	British Isles from Space
4–5	England and Wales
6	Scotland
7	Ireland
8	British Isles: Relief
9	British Isles: Counties and Regions

B

Manchester	4	D3	53 °N	2 °W
place or feature	*page*	*grid square*	*latitude*	*longitude*

C Satellite image of north-west England

Activities

1. Look at map **D** on page 7 and find the following features.

   - Manchester
   - Manchester airport
   - M6
   - The Pennines
   - The Peak
   - Blackpool
   - Ribble

2. Copy the table below. Complete it for the features listed in question 1. Manchester has been done for you.

Feature	Grid square	What is it?
Manchester	D3	A city
M6		

3. **a** Write the name of the place you live in as an atlas entry.

   b Choose two or more places that you know in other countries. Write out their atlas entries.

4. Use the satellite photograph **C** to find the places in question **1**.

5. **Extension**

   Find one feature that is shown on map **D**, but not on photo **C**. Can you suggest why it is not on the photo? Now find something on **C** that is not on **D**.

help!

C is a true-colour photo of part of the area shown in **D**. The brown areas are hills; the pinkish-grey areas show **settlements** and the green and yellow areas show **vegetation**.

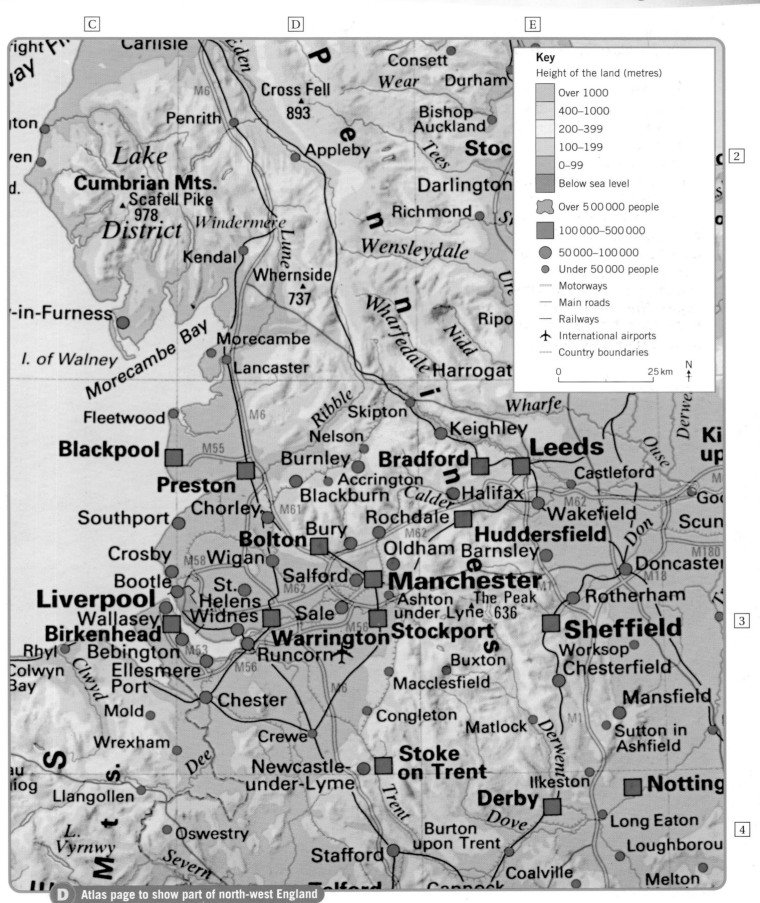

Key

Height of the land (metres)

	Over 1000
	400–1000
	200–399
	100–199
	0–99
	Below sea level

Over 5 00 000 people

100 000–500 000

50 000–100 000

Under 50 000 people

=== Motorways

— Main roads

— Railways

✈ International airports

--- Country boundaries

0   25 km

N

Carlisle
Consett
Wear   Durham
Cross Fell
893
Penrith
Appleby
Bishop Auckland
Stoc
Lake
Cumbrian Mts.
Scafell Pike
978
District
Windermere
Kendal
Darlington
Richmond
Wensleydale
Whernside
737
Wharfedale
-in-Furness
Morecambe Bay
Morecambe
Lancaster
Ripo
Nidd
I. of Walney
Harrogat
Fleetwood
Ribble
Skipton
Wharfe
Keighley
Blackpool
M6
Nelson
Bradford
Leeds
Ki
up
Preston
M55
Burnley
Accrington
Castleford
Chorley
Blackburn
Calder
Halifax
Goo
Southport
M61
Rochdale
Wakefield
Scun
Crosby
Bury
M62
Huddersfield
Don
M180
Bolton
Oldham
Barnsley
Doncaster
Bootle
Wigan
Salford
Manchester
M18
Liverpool
St.
M62
Ashton
The Peak
Rotherham
Wallasey
Helens
Widnes
Sale
under Lyne 636
Birkenhead
Warrington
Stockport
Sheffield
Rhyl
Bebington
Runcorn
Buxton
Worksop
Colwyn
Ellesmere
M56
Macclesfield
Chesterfield
Bay
Port
Chester
Congleton
Mansfield
Mold
Crewe
Matlock
M1
Sutton in
Wrexham
Dee
Newcastle-
Stoke
Ilkeston
Ashfield
under-Lyme
on Trent
Notting
Llangollen
Derby
Long Eaton
L.
Oswestry
Burton
Dove
Loughborou
Vyrnwy
Severn
upon Trent
Stafford
Coalville
Melton

C
D
E
2
3
4

Where are we?

Figure **A** is a photo of the world from a satellite. Actually, it is made up of lots of photos taken by a satellite as it circled the Earth. The Earth is a sphere, so it is impossible to see the whole surface at the same time. It is also impossible to draw it accurately on a flat piece of paper. To show the whole globe on a photo or a map, some parts have to be squashed and others stretched.

Lines of latitude are imaginary lines drawn around the Earth from east to west. The most famous line of latitude is the **Equator**. The Equator goes around the middle of the Earth. It is 0° and the other lines of latitude are measured in degrees north (° N) or degrees south (° S) of the Equator (see **B**).

Lines running north to south around the Earth are called **lines of longitude**. They are all the same length, and all of them pass through the North Pole and the South Pole. The line 0° of longitude passes through Greenwich in London. It is called the **Prime Meridian**. Other lines of longitude are numbered in degrees east (° E) or degrees west (° W) of the Prime Meridian (see **C**).

Every place has a latitude number and a longitude number, so that we can find that place on a map. Manchester's co-ordinates are 53 °N 2 °W. Each degree of latitude and longitude is also divided into 60 small sections called **minutes**, so that we can be even more accurate.

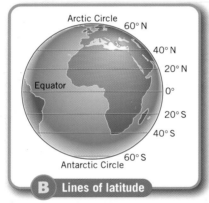

B Lines of latitude

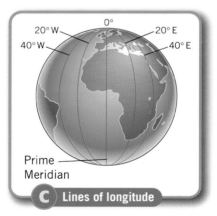

C Lines of longitude

Activity

① Copy out the table below. It shows the latitude and longitude of some places, including those in the photographs on pages 4 and 5. Use an atlas to complete the table.

Place	Latitude	Longitude	Place	Latitude	Longitude
Timbuktu	16°N		North Pole	90°N	0°E
New York		76°W	St Lucia	14°N	
River Amazon		50°W	Venice		12°E
Bombay	18°N		Sydney		
Mount Fuji	35°N		Salt Lake City		

Passport to the world

There are lots of places around the world that we have links to every day. This is a picture of Jenny sitting at home in her kitchen. The picture is labelled with some of the places she has had contacts with today.

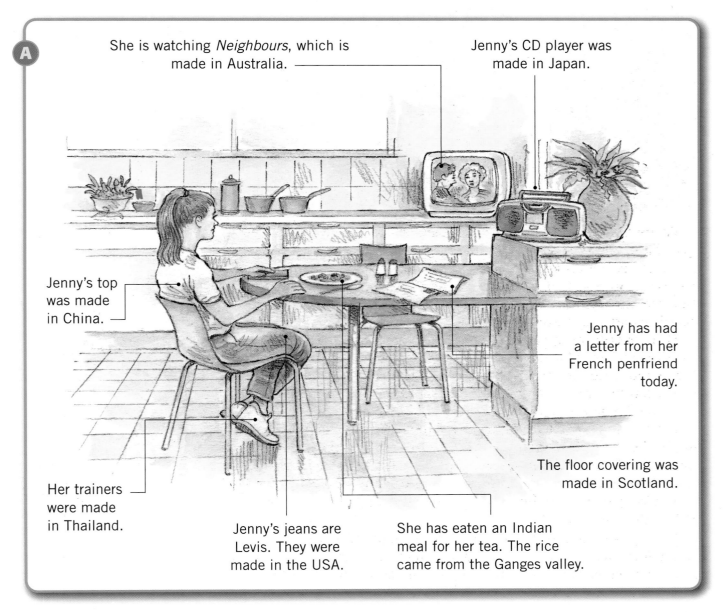

A

She is watching *Neighbours*, which is made in Australia.

Jenny's CD player was made in Japan.

Jenny's top was made in China.

Jenny has had a letter from her French penfriend today.

Her trainers were made in Thailand.

Jenny's jeans are Levis. They were made in the USA.

She has eaten an Indian meal for her tea. The rice came from the Ganges valley.

The floor covering was made in Scotland.

Activities

1 Make a list of all the places and countries which Jenny has had links with today. Mark them onto a world map. Use an atlas to help you.

2 Give your map a key and a title to include the words *linked*, *places*, *world*.

3 Make your own list of places in a world diary. Keep this diary for a month and then show all the places you have been linked to on a world map. Keep this list and the work you do with it in your World Passport.

Enquire within

The questions that geographers ask about people and places can often be answered by what they call an **enquiry** or investigation. When you carry out an enquiry there are a series of steps to follow. In the next pages you are going to learn about these steps and carry out an enquiry of your own.

Step 1: Asking questions

Geographers often carry out an enquiry to find out about a problem or issue in their local area. Sometimes they want to test a **hypothesis** (theory) or idea that they have about something. An enquiry may also be carried out to help people make a decision about something. For example, a company may have applied for planning permission to open a new fast food restaurant in your area. An enquiry question that you might like to ask is:

Why are fast food restaurants located where they are?

What sort of information do you need to help you make a decision about this?

Some questions you might like to ask include:

- What is fast food and what are fast food restaurants like?
- Who uses fast food restaurants and where do they come from?
- Is there a need for more fast food restaurants in the area?
- What effects do fast food restaurants have on the area around them?
- What alternatives are there to providing another restaurant?

How to ...

... ask geographical questions

Nearly all geographical questions will include at least one of the words:
- what?
- how?
- where?
- who?
- why?

If there are many things you want to ask about, you should ask several short questions.

A Inside a fast food restaurant

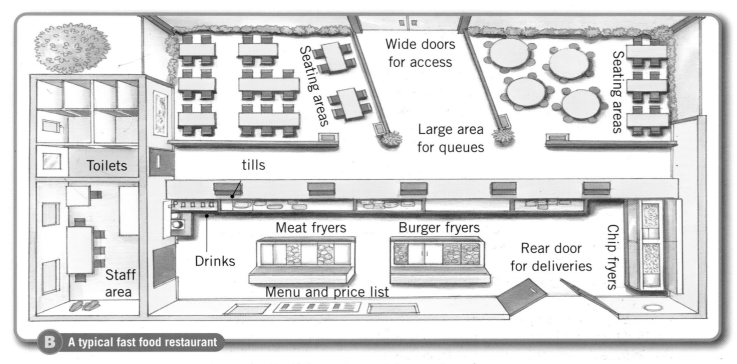

B A typical fast food restaurant

What are the features of a fast food restaurant?

The sketch in **A** above shows a typical fast food restaurant. There are several features that are common to fast food restaurants but which are not typical of other types of restaurants.

Activities

1 Copy the following table, which shows features of a fast food restaurant.
Give reasons to explain why restaurants have these features. The first one has been done for you. Then add some features of your own, and explanations for them.

Description	Explanation
Food is designed to be eaten without cutlery	*Saves washing up, so fewer people need to be employed*
Lots of tills	
Open-plan restaurants	
Several serving points	
Large signs on the outside of the restaurant	
A lot of disposable wrapping material	

2 Use the ideas you have collected to make a poster advertising a fast food restaurant, pointing out the features you have mentioned in your table. Your poster should try to persuade a group of people to come and eat at your restaurant. Choose from:

ⓢ school friends

ⓢ parents with young children

ⓢ single people who live alone.

You could use the desktop publishing software on your computer.

Step 2: Collecting information

Once you have decided which questions to ask, you must decide how you are going to find the answers to them. Some questions are easy to answer straight away. For others you need to find out more detailed information, from books, from visiting places or from asking other people questions. The information geographers can collect can be divided into two types:

- **Primary data** is information that you find out for yourself by looking, counting or asking people questions.

- **Secondary data** is information that you collect by looking at maps or books, or by using CD-ROMS or the Internet.

Collecting primary data using a questionnaire

Suppose that you want to find out about the types of fast food restaurants that your class likes to visit. You might choose to use a questionnaire, or you might want to make a survey of what types of restaurant are available in your town. You could investigate how far it is to the restaurants from each person's home, or which type of fast food your class likes best.

How to ...

... use a questionnaire

- Decide on the things you want to find out about.
- Try to ask questions which have answers that can be put into categories.
- Give some choices for people to give as an answer.
- Don't ask too many questions – people get bored!
- You could use a data-handling program to help you. **ICT**

Activities

① Some students have designed a questionnaire about fast food. Look at each question in **C**. Can you work out why the students asked each question?

---

1 **Do you like fast food?**   Yes ☐   No ☐

2 **If yes, what is your favourite fast food?**

Burgers ☐   Pizza ☐   Chicken ☐

Fish'n'chips ☐   Other ☐   Please name _____

3 **How far away from your home is your nearest fast food restaurant?**

Under 1 km ☐   1–3 km ☐   3–6 km ☐   more than 6 km ☐

4 **How often do you go to a fast food restaurant?**

More than once a week ☐   About once a month ☐

About once a week ☐   Less than once a month ☐

About once a fortnight ☐

5 **Which age group do you belong to?**

0–15 ☐   16–25 ☐   26–40 ☐   41–60 ☐   over 60 ☐

6 **Where do you live?**   In a town/city centre ☐

In the suburbs ☐   In the countryside ☐

Collecting secondary data using maps

Another way to collect information is by using maps. You could, for example, use a map to find out what types of fast food restaurants are available in your town or city. Map **D** shows the layout of a city centre.

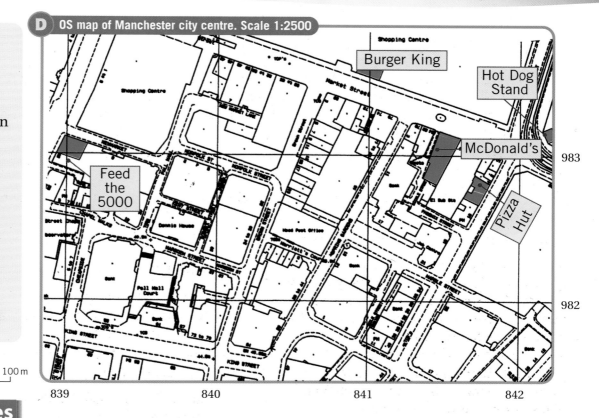

D OS map of Manchester city centre. Scale 1:2500

Burger King

Hot Dog Stand

McDonald's

Feed the 5000

Pizza Hut

0   100 m

839   840   841   842

983

982

Activities

❶ On a copy of map **D**, colour in all the fast food restaurants.

❷ Work out a route that allows you to visit all of them. Draw your route onto your map.

❸ Use the scale to work out how far you will have to walk. The instructions in the How to ... box will help you.

❹ Write a description of your route to tell someone else how to follow it.

❺ Are these statements true or false? Write out the correct ones.

◎ The fast food restaurants are a long way apart.

◎ The fast food restaurants are close together.

◎ The fast food restaurants are nearly all clustered together in the same location.

◎ The fast food restaurants are evenly spread out along the streets.

How to ...

... measure distances on a map

Measure the distance you have to travel by following these instructions.

1 Take a piece of paper with a straight edge.

2 Place the straight edge between the beginning and end of your journey.

3 Mark the two points on your piece of paper.

4 Move the paper to the scale line at the edge of the map.

5 With the first point on 0, read the distance you would have to travel on the scale line.

E Measuring distance on a map

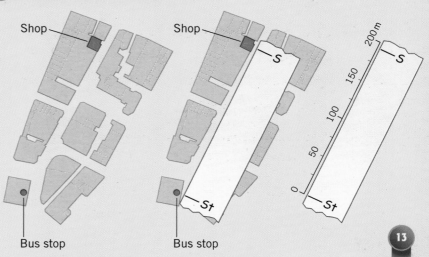

Shop

Shop

S

S

200 m

150

100

50

0

St

St

Bus stop

Bus stop

Step 3: Showing your results

Once you have collected your data, you need to change it from simple written answers and numbers into graphs, maps or diagrams. These should show the information in a more interesting way and make it easier to understand.

Investigating McDonald's in Great Britain

The first McDonald's restaurant opened in the USA in 1955. McDonald's opened its first UK restaurant in London in 1974. The restaurant proved to be very popular and the company opened more and more restaurants in the London area. Then, with an increase in demand between 1980 and 1984, the restaurants spread northwards to the Birmingham and Manchester regions. Today there are over 860 restaurants throughout Great Britain. Table **G** below shows how the restaurants have spread.

F A McDonald's fast food restaurant in Paris, France

Year	London	South-east England	Midlands	East Anglia	North-west England	North-east England	South-west England	Wales	Scotland	Total
1980	47	2	0	2	0	0	0	0	0	51
1988	106	32	46	20	46	24	2	10	8	294
1998	194	120	122	61	124	73	65	32	45	836

G McDonald's restaurants in Great Britain

1980

Key
restaurants
0
1–50
51–100
100+

0   300 km

1988

Key
restaurants
0
1–50
51–100
100+

0   300 km

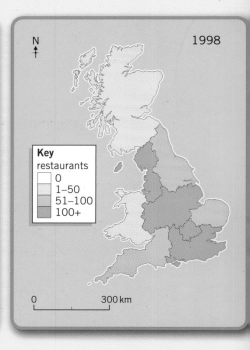

1998

Key
restaurants
0
1–50
51–100
100+

0   300 km

H This set of maps shows the growth of McDonald's restaurants in Great Britain since 1980

Activities

1 Use the information on page 14 to describe the growth of McDonald's in Great Britain. Use the writing frame on the right to help. 📖

2 Use blank copies of a map showing the regions of Great Britain. Draw graphs to show the distribution of restaurants, using the data from table **G**. ①②③

   a Using the data for 1980, make a bar chart, with a bar located in each region. (Each restaurant = 1 mm on the bar.)

   b Using the data for 1988, make a pictogram map. You could draw a picture – like a burger – for each one, where the size of each burger is equal to the number of restaurants. (The London burger could have a radius of 10.6 mm.)

   c Using the data for 1998, make a dot map of the information, following the instructions below.

3 Compare the maps and graphs you have drawn.

   a Which was the quickest to draw?

   b Which map or graph shows the information in the best way? Give reasons.

   c Can you think of any other ways you could have shown the information?

4 Compare your maps to map **I** of population distribution in Great Britain. Are there any similarities and differences between the maps?

Growth of McDonald's in Great Britain

In 1974 McDonald's opened its first restaurant in Great Britain. By 1980 there was a total of _____ restaurants, but most were in _____

By 1988 there were restaurants in _____

By 1998 the number of restaurants had grown to _____ and they could be found _____

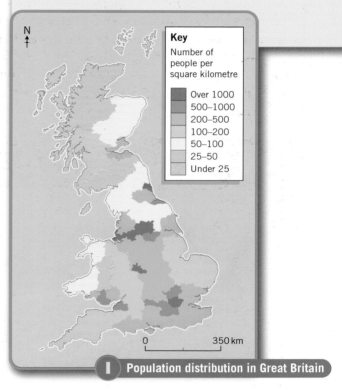

I Population distribution in Great Britain

How to ...

... draw a dot distribution map

1 You are going to show the distribution of McDonald's restaurants in 1998 on a map of Great Britain by drawing dots in each region.

2 Find the number of restaurants in the region from table **G**.

3 Use one dot for every ten restaurants:

   ◉ Divide the number of restaurants by 10.

   ◉ Give the number to the nearest 10; for London, 194/10 = 19.4 = 19 dots.

4 Draw the dots evenly over the region on your map.

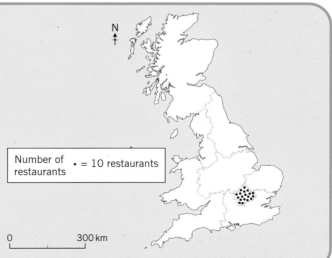

Investigating McDonald's around the world

McDonald's is a **transnational** company. This means that it does business all over the world.
In 2000, McDonald's had more than 26 000 restaurants worldwide in 119 countries on six continents.
This means that every minute of the day someone is eating a McDonald's for their lunch!

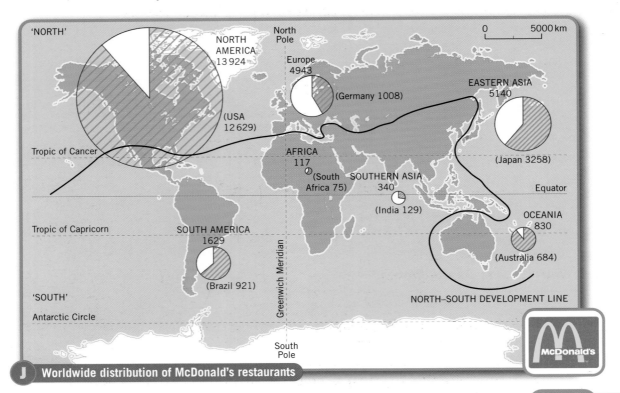

J **Worldwide distribution of McDonald's restaurants**

Map **J** shows some of the countries where McDonald's have restaurants. It also shows the total numbers of restaurants for each continent. The world has been divided into two by the **North–South Development Line**. This is an imaginary line. The richer MEDCs (more economically developed countries) are found to the north of the line, mainly in North America, Europe and Oceania. The poorer LEDCs (less economically developed countries) are found mainly in Asia, Africa and South America to the south of the line.

help!

Look at the 'How to…' on page 23 for help with describing patterns on maps.

Activities

1. Are there more McDonald's restaurants north or south of the **Development Line?** Can you suggest why this is so?

2. Use the writing frame to describe the distribution of the restaurants.

> **Worldwide distribution of McDonald's restaurants**
>
> McDonald's have some restaurants in the continents of _____
>
> They have very few restaurants in the continents of _____
>
> This is probably because_____
>
> On the other hand, there are many restaurants in the continents of _____
>
> In the USA _____ . This is probably because _____

Step 4: Drawing conclusions

By this stage in your enquiry you have collected all the information you need to answer your question. You have drawn graphs, maps and diagrams to display your results. You have explained what they show, and now you must come to some overall conclusions.

A conclusion:

◎ looks at all the work you have done

◎ links the results to the questions you asked at the beginning

◎ evaluates the strengths and weaknesses of the work as a whole

◎ makes suggestions about further investigations you might carry out.

Our main enquiry question was:

Why are fast food restaurants located where they are?

In your conclusion you should:

> *Give the features of a fast food restaurant.*
> *Say which you think are the most important.*

> *Describe the distribution of fast food restaurants in a town centre.*

> *Summarise the results of your questionnaire, saying what people think about fast food restaurants.*

> *Describe and give reasons for the distribution of McDonald's restaurants around the world.*

help!

You may want to start your conclusion something like this:

From our study of fast food restaurants it is clear that they have many features which make them different from other types of café or restaurant. The most important features are the things which allow the food to be served quickly and conveniently. For example, the restaurants have large service counters, lots of tills and plenty of space for people to queue…

Presenting your conclusions in different ways

A conclusion is not often the place where you present more graphs or maps. It is usually only writing. But sometimes it is possible to use a diagram or photograph which presents your information with more impact. The boxes show three ways of making your conclusions clearer.

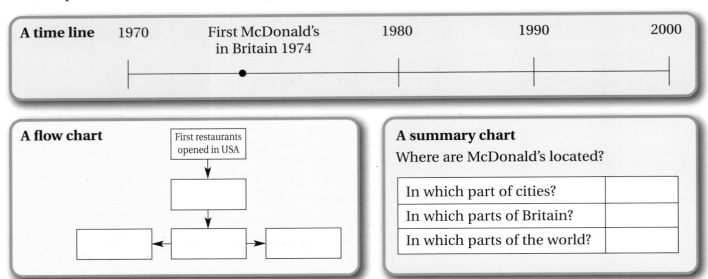

Evaluating your work

An **evaluation** of your work should finish off your enquiry.
It refers to the whole of the project and should look at the *strengths*, such as:

- what you found most interesting or useful in your work
- what you think went well.

It also looks at the *weaknesses*:

- the problems or difficulties you had collecting information
- if it would have been better to collect more or different information.

You can also suggest ideas for further investigations:

- Would a study of another fast food chain like Wimpy or Harry Ramsden's give you the same results?
- In what ways would the locations of Drive-thru restaurants be different?

Activities

Research activity

1 What do we know, think and feel about other places?

   a Choose a place mentioned in this unit that you would like to visit.

   b Find out all you can about it. Use all the resources you have used in this unit, such as atlases, newspapers, CD-ROMS, Internet and textbooks. (ICT)

   c Prepare a brochure for tourists telling them what the place is like. Illustrate it with pictures, maps and diagrams.

Review and reflect

Activities

1 You can now use all the things you have learned about in this unit to carry out an investigation about the place where you live. Follow the route to enquiry:

1 **Asking questions** – How is our place connected to other places?

2 **Collecting information** – make up a questionnaire to ask people you know about the connections they have with other places. You could ask where their parents were born, where they go on holiday, or where they shop. *Use the work you did on page 12 to help you with this.*

3 **Showing your results** – use the results of your survey to make maps and diagrams to show what you have found out. Write a description of what they show. *Look back at the writing frames used to describe patterns on pages 15–16.*

4 **Drawing conclusions** – look back at the original question and explain what you have found out about your place's connections to other places. Remember to say what part of your enquiry went well and what part could have been improved. *Some ideas for this were given on page 18.*

Things you have learned about	Pages	Examples
Using an atlas		Finding places in north-west England
Measuring distances on maps		Finding how far to walk between restaurants in a city centre
Finding places using latitude and longitude	8–9	Giving the location of the pictures
Planning routes on maps		
Describing patterns on maps		
Drawing annotated sketches		
Carrying out an enquiry		

2 Make a large copy of the table. Fill in the things you have learned about or done for each of the parts of this unit. Examples have been given to help you.

3 Write down three skills that you developed or improved in doing this unit. Explain how these might be useful later on in your geography studies.

4 Write down two things that you learned in this unit and that you did not know before.

5 Write down any activities you found difficult, and say why.

2 Restless Earth

Earthquakes and volcanoes

Learn about

A volcanic eruption or an earthquake can be disastrous, especially if it is in a place where many people live. Understanding the causes and effects of volcanoes and earthquakes can help people to manage the problems that they cause. In this unit you will learn:

- what volcanoes and earthquakes are and where they occur
- what happens when a volcano erupts
- how volcanic eruptions affect different places in the world in different ways
- what happens in an earthquake
- how people can try to reduce the effects of earthquakes
- how aid can help earthquake and volcano victims
- why people want to live in active zones.

Activities

Discussion activity

1. Look carefully at the photographs on these two pages.

   a Which do you think are about **earthquakes** and which are about **volcanoes**? What are your reasons for thinking this?

   b For each photograph, agree on at least two things it tells you about earthquakes or volcanoes.

   c Do the photographs show the *causes* or the *effects* of earthquakes and volcanoes?

2. These are all dramatic or negative images about earthquakes and volcanoes. What positive effects do you think earthquakes and volcanoes can have on people and places?

3. Start to create a word bank of the key words and terms you have used – begin with *earthquake*, *volcano*, *cause* and *effect*.

Where do volcanoes and earthquakes occur?

Activities

Research activity

1 Find out about volcanoes from around the world that have **erupted** since 1900. You could use a CD-ROM or a website on the Internet, such as http://volcano.und.nodak.edu. Use the information to create a fact file like the one below. (ICT)

Volcano location	Volcano name	Year of eruption	Latitude and longitude		Height
Philippines	Mayon	2000	13°N	123°E	2462 m
Montserrat, West Indies	Soufriere Hills	1999	16°N	62°W	915 m
Sicily, Italy	Etna	1999	37°N	15°E	3350 m
Mexico	Popocatepetl	1999	19°N	98°W	5465 m

2 Find out about earthquakes from around the world since 1900. You could use a CD-ROM or a website on the Internet, such as http://wwwneic.cr.usgs.gov. Use the information to create a fact file like the one below. (ICT)

Earthquake location	Year	Latitude and longitude		Magnitude (strength)
Taiwan	2000	26°N	124°E	6.0
Japan	2000	40°N	143°E	4.5
Iran	1999	28°N	57°E	6.5
Fiji	1998	15°S	179°W	6.7
Mexico	1995	19°N	104°W	8.0
Chile	1995	23°S	70°W	8.0
India	1950	28°N	96°E	8.6

3 Plot the volcanoes and earthquakes from your fact files onto a world map. Choose one symbol for volcanoes and a different one for earthquakes.

4 Draw a key and give the map a title that includes these words: *world, location, volcanoes, earthquakes*.

5 Write down definitions for the following words in your glossary: *location, erupt, magnitude*.

In geography, we can put the **location** of different things on a map. When lots of things are located, there is sometimes a pattern on the Earth's surface. Have a look at the map below. It shows some of the world's strongest earthquakes and volcanoes. Can you **describe** the pattern?

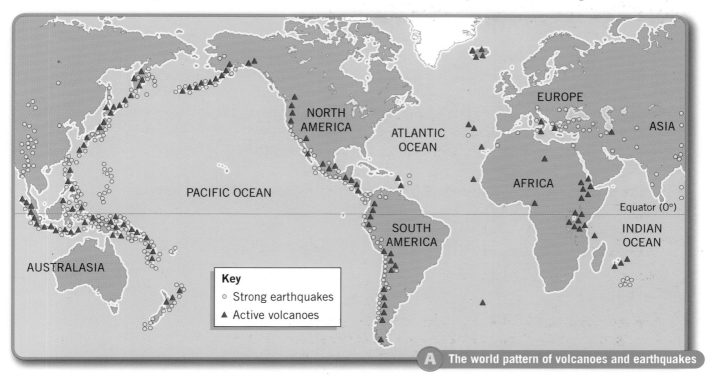

Key
○ Strong earthquakes
▲ Active volcanoes

A The world pattern of volcanoes and earthquakes

Activities

1 Copy the paragraph below to describe the world pattern of volcanoes. Choose the correct word to complete each sentence.

The map shows that many volcanoes are found in a big circle around the Pacific/Atlantic Ocean. There are many volcanoes on South America's east/west coast and the islands of Asia/Europe. Africa has a few volcanoes, but some places seem to have none at all, for example Europe/Australia.

2 Now write one sentence to **describe** the distribution of earthquakes.

   ◎ First write a general statement
   ◎ Add one piece of detail and some places
   ◎ Try to mention at least one direction

3 Write a definition of the word **describe** in your glossary.

How to ...

... describe patterns on maps

◎ Begin with a **general statement**, e.g. *'The map shows that volcanoes and earthquakes are found ...'.*

◎ Go on to give greater **detail** about where in the world they are and are not found.

◎ Include **place names**, e.g. *countries, continents, seas, oceans, mountain ranges ...*

◎ Mention **directions** for the patterns: *... north to south, ... to the south-west,* etc.

Why do volcanoes and earthquakes occur where they do?

The Earth's surface is a thin crust. This crust is made up of big chunks, called **tectonic plates**, which move slowly around in different directions. Some plates, like the **North American** and **Eurasian Plates** are moving away from one another. Others, like the **Nazca** and **South American Plates**, are moving towards each other,

and crashing. Finally, in some parts of the world, the plates are sliding sideways past each other, as along the **San Andreas Fault** in the western USA. The edges of the tectonic plates are called **active zones**, because this is where active earthquakes and volcanoes are found.

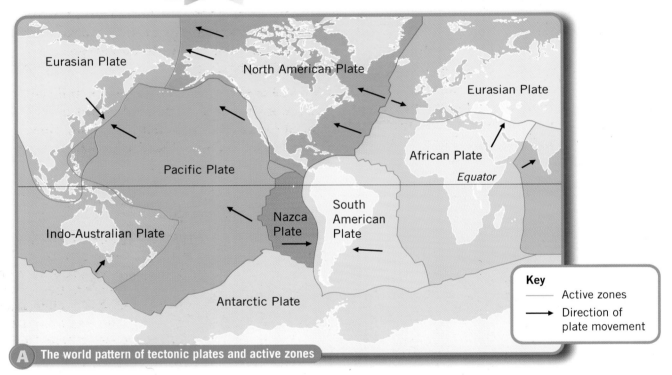

A The world pattern of tectonic plates and active zones

Activities

❶ Match the earthquakes and volcanoes with active zones, by comparing two maps: map **A** on page 23 with map **A** above. Copy and complete Table **B** below.

Active zone	What you find	Example
Where tectonic plates move apart	Lots of volcanoes	The middle of the Atlantic Ocean
Where tectonic plates crash together		
Where tectonic plates slide past one another		

❷ Look again at the maps and your table. What does your table prove? Copy and complete this sentence: The table shows that earthquakes and volcanoes tend to happen where _____

What are volcanoes?

Volcanoes are openings (**vents**) in the Earth's crust where **magma** (molten rock) from inside the Earth is able to escape to the surface. The magma can appear in a number of different forms:

- as liquid **lava** (molten rock) that flows down the volcano sides

- as **volcanic bombs** – lumps of molten rock that solidify as they fall from the sky

- as hot ash and dust which are thrown into the air and eventually settle on the surrounding land

- as steam and gases, which may be poisonous.

Volcanic eruptions are strongly influenced by the type of magma that escapes. Some are very explosive and dangerous. When Mount Pinatubo in the Philippines erupted in 1991, it sent up a cloud of ash and steam 30 km high. About 700 people died as a result of the eruption.

Other eruptions are more gentle. Kilauea, one of the Hawaiian Islands, has been continuously pouring out runny lava since 1983 with little threat to humans.

Volcanoes may be active, dormant or extinct.

- **Active volcanoes** are those that have erupted within historical time and are likely to erupt again. There are over 700 active volcanoes in the world.

- **Dormant volcanoes** are inactive now but may erupt again. Most of the Cascade volcanoes on the west coast of North America are believed to be dormant.

- **Extinct volcanoes** are those that are unlikely to erupt again in the future. There are a number of extinct volcanoes in Britain, such as the one Edinburgh Castle is built on.

A Volcanic eruption on the island of Heimaey, Iceland

Activity

1. Make a large copy of the sketch below. Put these labels in the right place on it. Look at photo **A** to find where they are. Two have been done to help you.

   - Volcano
   - Sea
   - Buildings
   - Lava
   - Hill
   - Ash and dust

What happens when a volcano erupts?

The Philippine Islands are located in an active zone on the edges of the Eurasian and Philippine Plates. This active zone is part of the 'Pacific Ring of Fire' where there are many volcanoes and earthquakes. Mount Pinatubo is one of 22 active volcanoes in the Philippines and is located about 100 km north-west of the capital city, Manila. After being dormant for more than 600 years, Pinatubo awoke with a bang on 9 June 1991. It caused one of the largest eruptions of the twentieth century.

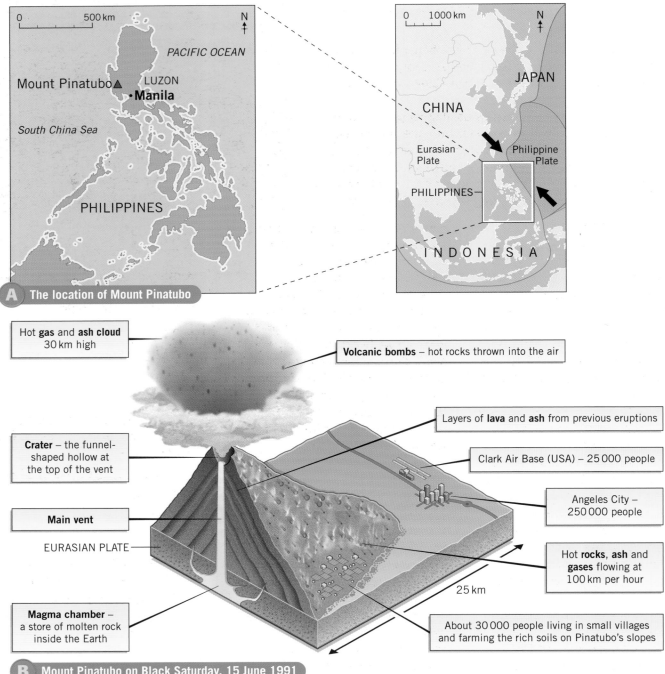

A The location of Mount Pinatubo

Hot **gas** and **ash cloud** 30 km high

Volcanic bombs – hot rocks thrown into the air

Crater – the funnel-shaped hollow at the top of the vent

Main vent

EURASIAN PLATE

Magma chamber – a store of molten rock inside the Earth

Layers of **lava** and **ash** from previous eruptions

Clark Air Base (USA) – 25 000 people

Angeles City – 250 000 people

Hot **rocks, ash** and **gases** flowing at 100 km per hour

25 km

About 30 000 people living in small villages and farming the rich soils on Pinatubo's slopes

B Mount Pinatubo on Black Saturday, 15 June 1991

The eruption of Mount Pinatubo

Extracts from the diary of Kimi Nath

C **The eruption of Mount Pinatubo**

When the Angeles City newspapers reported that a group of American volcano scientists had moved into the Clark Air Base, everyone was talking about Mount Pinatubo and saying, 'What volcano?' Many Filipinos had never heard of the volcano, which had been dormant for over 600 years.

Wednesday 12 June

Mount Pinatubo gave us the first taste of her fury. A deep, rumbling boom shook the earth, and an angry, dark cloud appeared in the distance. A cold wind blew around us. It was very eerie.

As the 'cloud' moved towards us, it spread out and the sun disappeared. Dust began to fall from the sky. By the time the 'cloud' drifted past us, 2 cm of ash coated the ground. The same thing happened on Thursday, and on Friday. Everyone was tense, wondering what would happen next. We didn't have to wait long before we found out.

D **Ash on the cars at Clark Air Base**

Saturday 15 June

The sun was shining brightly at 8.30 a.m. After clearing 5 to 6 cm of ash from my car, I drove to the Clark Air Base, just north of Angeles City, for a meeting. Around 9.00 a.m. a huge rumble shook the room, and the sky began to darken. By 9.30 it was midnight black. By a cruel twist of fate, a huge typhoon hit at the same time. Swirling winds mixed the heavy rain with ash so that mud fell from the sky. The force of the eruption was so strong that huge pieces of the volcano blew apart, so that rocks also rained down. Electricity, water and telephones all failed, so we sat in darkness. The muddy ash came down more heavily with each passing moment, and the 'rotten eggs' stench from the sulphur in the air made us sick. Sulphur fireballs shot blazing orange through the night, and the typhoon brought lightning, which exploded in fiery displays. Then the earthquakes began ... They came one after another, shifting the ground beneath us. Some were powerful enough to send things crashing to the ground and to crack the beams of the homes in which we huddled. With the awful storm outside and the earthquakes within, there was no safe place to go. Throughout 'Black Saturday' we huddled in fear and wondered if the world was truly coming to an end.

Sunday 16 June

We came out of our shelters cautiously and looked in awe on the grey devastation all around us. Our homes were buried in ash and hundreds of buildings had collapsed. Roads were blocked by mud, trees and vehicles; the power was still off and there wasn't much food or water. We knew things were never going to get back to normal ...

Activity

1 Kimi Nath describes what happened in the eruption. Write down one thing that Kimi Nath could:

- see
- hear
- smell
- feel.

2 Give two other things that the volcano did to make everyday life difficult for people.

- *It made it too dark to go out during the day.*

3 Give two other things that the volcano did to endanger human life.

- *Falling rocks could have killed people.*

Pinatubo leaves behind a wasteland

Pinatubo's ash, dust and **lahars** (mudflows) have turned vast areas of farmland into a wasteland. Warnings meant that 14 000 people were evacuated, but more than 249 000 families (1.2 million people) were still affected by the eruption. 700 people died and 184 were injured.

Water supplies, power lines, roads and bridges were badly damaged by the lahars. Houses and public buildings collapsed under the weight of ash and planes could not use the Clark Air Base. Even Manila International Airport, 100 km away, was closed for four days.

F Extract from *The Philippine Star*, 21 July 1991

G Mount Pinatubo's new crater lake, formed after the 1991 eruption

H Whole villages were covered in ash

Lahars swept away whole villages. Green rice paddies and sugar-cane fields were covered with ash. About 4000 square kilometres were affected, but people have since returned to farm the rich soils formed from the mud and ash.

I

Pinatubo's eruption threw 20 million tonnes of sulphur dioxide into the air. Scientists think that this caused a 1°C fall in global temperatures for over five years. The dust thrown into the atmosphere by Pinatubo may also add to global warming in the future.

J

Wildlife returns to Mount Pinatubo

Eight years after Pinatubo's hot gases stripped its trees of life and ash blanketed its slopes, wild cats, boars, deer and monkeys are returning to areas where plants have started to grow again. Snakes, such as boa constrictors and cobras, and even monitor lizards are also appearing on the volcano's slopes.

K Extract from article by Ding Cervantes, 20 April 1999

This **satellite image** of the area around Mount Pinatubo was taken by the space shuttle Endeavour on 13 April 1994. The main **crater** and its lake can easily be seen in *blue*. The *pale pink* colour on the slopes of Pinatubo shows the ash deposited during the 1991 eruption. The *dark pink* areas show the lahars. These are still a hazard to the people who have returned to farm the area around the volcano. Every time rain falls on Mount Pinatubo, mud slides down from the highlands *(dark green)* on to villages, homes and fields. On the western side of the image the lahars spill into the South China Sea *(black)*. Satellite images can be very helpful in monitoring hazards such as lahars. This can stop lives being lost.

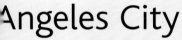
A 'false-colour' satellite image of the area around Pinatubo

Angeles City
– well on the road to recovery

Over 250 000 people lost their jobs as a result of the eruption of Mount Pinatubo in 1991. The American Clark Air Base was closed, and with it went thousands of jobs as local businesses, such as restaurants and taxi firms also closed.

Angeles City

Then Angeles started to grow as a tourist destination, with visitors coming to see the site of the eruption. It now has twenty-four restaurants, six new hotels, thirty nightclubs, four Internet cafes and hundreds of small tourist shops. The tourist industry is now the largest employer, with thousands of jobs for local Filipinos. The government is spending large sums of money to attract foreign tourists.

help!

When you write your brochure, remember that good geographers:

- include specific facts, figures and place names in their work
- write information in their own words
- evaluate their work when it is finished.

Activity

A tourist guide can earn P300 for each tour that they take up Mount Pinatubo. The Angeles Tourist Information Office has asked you to produce a brochure for visitors. The brochure must have the following:

1 A **location map** based on the satellite image above.
- Write labels for the volcano and the South China Sea.
- Draw, shade and label the volcano crater, the lake, ash and lahars.
- Provide a scale, a key and a title.

2 A **cross section diagram**, like **B** on page 26.
- Draw and label the diagram to show what happened in the eruption.

3 A **written explanation** of what happened and why.
Include these words and phrases:

9th June 1991   600 years   trees

dormant

roads   ash   volcanic bombs   farms

lahars

buildings   the world's climate   plates

local people   active zone   volcano

Remember that the brochure needs to look good, so include pictures or illustrations. Also remember that tourists might not know some of the terms, so provide a glossary of any difficult words.

What happens in an earthquake?

The Earth is made up of three main layers – the **crust**, the **mantle** and the **core**. The crust is much thinner than the other layers and is the only layer of the Earth that humans have actually seen. The Earth's crust is made up of huge chunks, called **tectonic plates**. These plates move around slowly in different directions. Earthquakes and volcanoes usually happen when two tectonic plates move past one another. This is why the edges of the tectonic plates are called **active zones**.

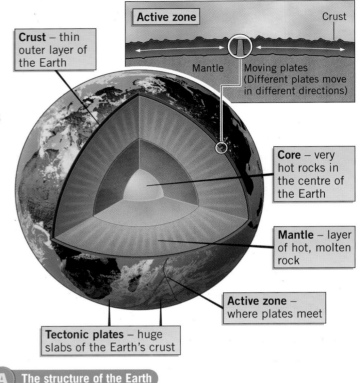

Crust – thin outer layer of the Earth

Active zone

Crust

Mantle

Moving plates (Different plates move in different directions)

Core – very hot rocks in the centre of the Earth

Mantle – layer of hot, molten rock

Active zone – where plates meet

Tectonic plates – huge slabs of the Earth's crust

A The structure of the Earth

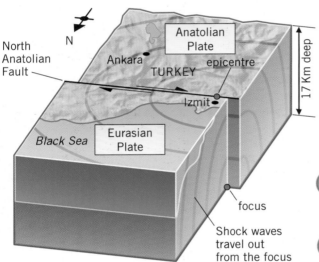

North Anatolian Fault

N

Ankara

Anatolian Plate

TURKEY

epicentre

Izmit

Black Sea

Eurasian Plate

17 Km deep

focus

Shock waves travel out from the focus

B The Izmit earthquake in Turkey, 17 August 1999

Earthquakes are caused when two plates moving past one another become 'stuck' for a while so that tension builds up. Eventually the stress becomes so great that the crust breaks and moves suddenly. The point where the rock actually breaks is called the **focus**. This is usually found far beneath the surface of the Earth. The point on the surface directly above the focus is called the **epicentre**. When the plates move suddenly, **shock waves** are sent out in all directions. These waves can cause a lot of damage on the Earth's surface.

The strength of an earthquake is measured using an instrument called a seismograph which records the shaking of the ground. Look at the seismogram **C** for the Turkish earthquake in 1999. The strength is shown by

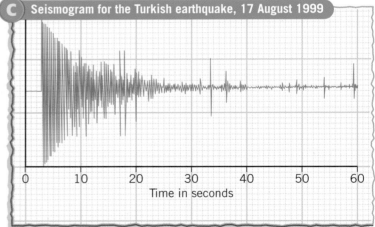

C Seismogram for the Turkish earthquake, 17 August 1999

Time in seconds

the lines that go up and down. The stronger the quake, the longer will be the lines drawn on the graph. The length of time that a quake lasts is shown by the horizontal distance across the graph.

The strength of an earthquake can be measured using the **Richter Scale** (see **D**). Earthquakes below 2.5 are not usually felt by humans.

Activities

1 Copy out the passage below. Use the word box to fill in the gaps and explain what happened in the Izmit earthquake.

A huge earthquake measuring _____ on the Richter Scale happened in Turkey on 17 August 1999. It was caused when two plates, the _____ Plate and the _____ Plate, became 'stuck' for a while. This caused stress to build up until the Earth's crust eventually broke, sending out _____ in all directions. The focus of the earthquake was about _____ km below the Earth's surface. The earthquake lasted for about _____ seconds and was most violent during the first _____ seconds.

The epicentre of the earthquake was near the city of _____ .

Word box

Eurasian	Izmit	shock waves	Anatolian
40	17	7.4	20

2 Write a sentence to explain why Izmit is a dangerous place to live. Try to use some of these words: **earthquake   active zone   epicentre   tectonic plates**.

Research activities

3 Find the name of a scale, other than the Richter Scale, which is used to measure earthquakes.

4 Download a map from the Internet showing the most recent earthquakes in the world. Use one of the following sites:

http://www.geo.arizona.edu

http://wwwneic.cr.usgs.gov

a Draw a table like the one on the right. Fill in the details for each earthquake.

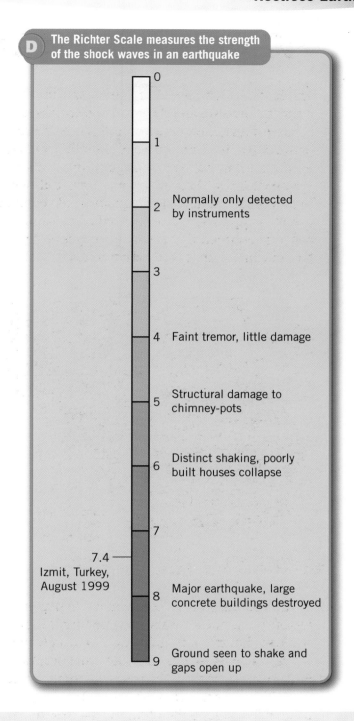

D The Richter Scale measures the strength of the shock waves in an earthquake

- 2 Normally only detected by instruments
- 4 Faint tremor, little damage
- 5 Structural damage to chimney-pots
- 6 Distinct shaking, poorly built houses collapse
- 7.4 Izmit, Turkey, August 1999
- 8 Major earthquake, large concrete buildings destroyed
- 9 Ground seen to shake and gaps open up

b Give the table a suitable title.

Country	Date

c Most of these earthquakes were not on our TV news. Why do you think that they were not reported? Give two different reasons.

How do earthquakes affect people and places?

A

B

C

D

E

F

Activities

Look at the photos on this page and the earthquake pictures on pages 20 and 21. They give you some ideas about the different ways that earthquakes affect people and the places they live. Use the photos to answer these questions. Try to add your own ideas as well.

1 Make a copy of the table below. Write three more sentences in each column.

How earthquakes affect places where people live (e.g. buildings, transport, electricity supplies)	How earthquakes affect people
Hospitals might collapse because of the shaking	People might be trapped under the rubble

2 Compare your list with another person's list. Add two more ideas to your own.

3 Now decide which is the worst effect on **places** (column 1) and the worst effect on **people** (column 2). Put a * next to each one.

4 Explain why each of these is the worst. Start your sentence like this:

I think that the worst effect on a place is when an earthquake _____ . This is because _____ .

The worst thing that an earthquake can do to people is _____ . This is because _____ .

After the Earthquake

Whether to cry out in answer to
My father's strangled cries
As he shifts bricks above my head,
Or whether to keep silent, holding back
This dust with clamped lips. I lie   5
Sealed in and cannot choose.

If I speak, death will steal my breath,
Seeping in at the mouth;
If I choose silence he may go away
And weep, and never know how close   10
My grave, how I longed to answer.

Someone flutes powder from my face.
I feel warm breath. My eyelids move:
Their flutter fills my eyes with grit.
Weight lifts from chest and arms   15
And inch by inch I live again.

In my father's arms
I cannot find strength to haul up
Words from my darkness.

by Angela Topping

Activities

1 Read the poem above and, working together in a small group, try to answer the questions in the table below.

Question	Answer	Evidence from the poem
Who has 'written' the poem?	A child	It says 'my father' in line 2
Where is the child trapped?		
Why can the child not speak or shout out?		
Why does the child want to speak or shout?		
Are the child's eyes open?		
Is the child rescued?		

2 What would it be like to be trapped for a whole day under the rubble? Write three words, which are <u>not</u> in the poem, that you would feel if you were trapped for a whole day. Explain why you chose these words.

3 Now write a poem of your own, written from the father's viewpoint. Imagine how he feels when he is looking for his child in the rubble. Copy the boxes below to plan the words for your poem.

Lines 1–5	**Lines 6–10**	**Lines 11–15**
panic ?	scratch scrabble	tears ?

At first what does he think, see, hear, feel?

Then what does he do?

In the end, what happens and how does he feel?

?   ?   ?   ?   ?   ?

Case Study

What happened in the 1999 earthquake in Turkey?

On Tuesday 17 August 1999 at 3 a.m. a strong earthquake hit north-west Turkey. Its epicentre was close to the city of Izmit, 55 km south-east of Istanbul (see map A).

A The location of the earthquake

B The North Anatolian Fault

The earthquake's epicentre was about 11 km south-east of the city of Izmit. It was caused by the movement of the Eurasian Plate (moving east) and the Anatolian Plate (moving west) in an active zone known as the North Anatolian Fault (see map **B**). In places the plates moved up to 5 metres in opposite directions. The effects of this could be seen on roads and railways that crossed the North Anatolian Fault (see photo **D**).

The earthquake measured 7.4 on the Richter Scale. It was a shallow earthquake, just 17 km below the Earth's surface. Shallow earthquakes do more damage than deeper ones because there is less of the Earth's crust above them to absorb the force of the shock waves.

Report from The National Earthquake Information Centre

C

D A railway crossing the North Anatolian Fault

Terror in Turkey: quake kills more than 2000

The worst recorded earthquake to hit Turkey killed at least 2000 people and injured thousands today. It destroyed buildings and cut off power and water to millions living in the area.

The quake struck at 3 o'clock this morning, while most people were still asleep. The lucky ones ran into the street in panic; others were crushed in the rubble. Many fled their homes in nightclothes and without shoes.

Dozens of buildings and highway overpasses collapsed in Istanbul, and many roads were severely damaged and unusable.

With the city's rescue services stretched to the limit, it was mostly neighbours and relatives who fought to pull people from the wreckage.

Local people working under car headlights in the early hours used their bare hands to try to dig people out of the rubble, while the young and elderly slept in the open.

The USA, France, Germany, Switzerland, Italy, Japan and Israel have all offered help, but rescue teams with special equipment and sniffer dogs will take time to get to Turkey.

E News report, 17 August 1999

Dead	Injured	People homeless	People living on the streets
15 135	23 983	600 000	200 000

F Casualty assessment report by Government Crisis Centre, 6 September 1999

Place	Date	Magnitude	Deaths
Turkey	1999	7.4	15 135
Afghanistan	1998	7.1	5000
Afghanistan	1998	6.4	4000
Iran	1997	7.1	1613
Russia	1995	7.5	1841
Japan	1995	7.2	6424
India	1993	6.4	7801
Indonesia	1992	6.8	2000
India	1991	6.1	1500
Afghanistan	1991	6.8	1500
Philippines	1990	7.7	1641
Iran	1990	7.7	40 000

G The worst earthquakes of the 1990s

I heard a deep thump and a few seconds later the whole house started shaking like crazy. We had a hard time running down the stairs, getting tossed from one side to the other. It did not stop for 45 seconds. When we reached the garden I saw the water in the swimming pool getting splashed around as if a ship was going through it. Tiles around the pool were shooting 1-2 metres up into the air. Then it stopped.

Minutes after the quake the entire city was without power. I saw a starry sky for the first time in more than a decade as the city was in total darkness, apart from the headlights of the cars driving around aimlessly ...

Kadir Bahcecik, Istanbul

H E-mail sent to a website for those wishing to contact family and friends after the earthquake

Activities

1 Look at the news report **E**. There is a photo with the report, but what would make a better picture for the news story? Sketch your own image of the Izmit earthquake using details from the text.

2 **a** In article **E**, how many people does it say died?
b In table **F**, how many people does it say died?
c Suggest why the two numbers are different.

3 Look at **G**. How many earthquakes in the 1990s were more powerful than the Izmit one? Did the more powerful ones kill more people? Can you explain your answer?

'I have been crying for two nights and no one has come to save my family,' shouted Mehmet, as he burst into the mayor's office with tears streaming down his face. 'If you don't come to my house soon, I will dynamite it myself to free them!' Anger, desperation and grief had carved deep lines around his mouth. He, like thousands of others, can't understand why there isn't a crane on every heap of rubble searching for those still missing.

I Television news report, 20 August 1999

SHODDILY BUILT HOUSES COLLAPSE IN QUAKE

There has been growing public anger that so many buildings fell down because precautions against earthquakes had not been taken.

In recent years, officials have turned a blind eye to builders who have skimped on materials to provide housing for the flood of people moving in from the countryside.

In the town of Duzce, 33 people thought to be responsible for the collapse of several buildings have been arrested. One of them admitted to mixing salty sea water with concrete. This caused buildings to crumble when the quake hit.

Buildings constructed over the past five years, using Turkey's earthquake building code, seem to have survived the quake much better.

J Newspaper report, 23 August 1999

40 000 FEARED DEAD IN TURKISH QUAKE

Fears are growing that the death toll from Turkey's devastating earthquake could eventually reach 40 000, making it the country's worst this century.

More than 10 000 people are already known to have died and another 45 000 people have been injured. The Turkish authorities are predicting that thousands more bodies will be found beneath the rubble.

Rescuers breaking iron bars to reach a trapped woman

Concern is growing for the health of those who have lived through the quake, with disease the latest threat to survivors. The fear of aftershocks has persuaded millions of people to camp out in the open – close to the rotting bodies of those killed in the earthquake. 'The greatest problem now facing us is that of disease,' Prime Minister Ecevit told reporters.

Most rescue workers are wearing masks, and are being immunised against typhoid. Cholera cases are being reported in some areas.

K Newspaper report, 20 August 1999

Activities

1 Look at **I** and **K**. These reports were written three days after the earthquake, on 20th August.

- Why was everyone not rescued by then?
- How many people did they think might die?
- Give two things that might still kill people.

2 Look at report **J**, written on 23rd August. Explain why people were now angry.

3 After people had been rescued, there was still lots to do. Look at **J** and the other reports on page 37.

a Find three things that the Turkish Government must do.

b Put your list in order, like this:

By 27th August, the most urgent thing to do was to _____ .

It was also urgent to _____

Another priority was to _____ .

c Compare your list with another person. Do they agree with you?

The earthquake damaged buildings from Istanbul to Bolu (a distance of 250 km). Nearly 70 per cent of the buildings in the cities of Golcuk, Izmit, Topcular and Kular fell down. Most deaths and injuries were caused by collapsing buildings.

While most buildings were damaged by the shaking of the ground, on the coast waves rushed in as the ground sank and washed houses into the sea. Many of the collapsed buildings were four to eight storeys high and built of reinforced concrete.

Buildings collapsed as a result of:

- poor concrete quality
- poor reinforcement
- building alterations (e.g. an added floor)
- badly prepared building sites.

It will cost about £3.4 billion to rebuild the destroyed buildings.

L **Report by the Earthquake Engineering Research Institute**

Winter thoughts weigh heavily on the homeless

Ankle-deep in mud, in tent cities swamped by rain, homeless quake survivors wonder whether they will have a sturdy roof over their heads by winter, now just two months away. Unfortunately, the odds are against them – 600 000 people have been left homeless. Although the government has announced the building of 200 000 new homes, these will take up to three years to complete. People whose houses are declared safe have been asked to return home.

M **Newspaper report, 27 August 1999**

N **Newspaper report, September 1999**

NEW SYSTEMS CONSIDERED

Mindful of dangers from new quakes, Turkey has been considering new preparation measures. The *Milliyet* newspaper reported today that the government would spend £2 million on an early-warning system for Istanbul, a city of 12 million people.

It said the system would provide an early warning of shock waves, allow damaged buildings to be checked quickly, and help to prevent gas leaks that could cause fires.

Activities

1. Write a script for a five-minute TV news report on '*Why did so many people die in the Turkish earthquake?*' Your report is to be broadcast one month after the earthquake. Write your report in four sections.

   - What happened in the earthquake – the **facts and figures** and the **effects** on people and places.
   - The **cause** of the earthquake – why it happened there.
   - The **responses** of the government and the emergency services.
   - How the Turkish government plans to **prevent** so many deaths next time.

2. Begin each section of the report with an enquiry question. For example, the first section might start with:

   What happened on August 17th?

3. Your report should also contain:

   - location maps at different scales, labelled with information about the earthquake
   - eye-catching graphs and diagrams showing relevant data
   - memorable images (such as photographs)
   - stories about 'real' people affected by the earthquake – these help to capture the imagination of the viewers.

help!

Good geographers:

- think carefully about the best ways of presenting information
- write information in their own words
- alter the way information is presented, e.g. change tables into graphs or maps
- annotate or label maps, photographs and diagrams
- carry out their own research into enquiry questions.

How can people make earthquakes less of a hazard?

Since 1900 nearly 3 million people have been killed by earthquakes. Scientists still cannot say exactly when or where an earthquake will strike. Successful earthquake **prediction** is very rare. In San Francisco, USA, in 1989 and Kobe, Japan, in 1995, the quakes came without any real warning. One famous example of prediction was in China in 1976 when local people in Haicheng reported early-warning signs. People camped outside and survived the quake that followed. In some parts of the world people can make earthquakes less of a hazard by making careful plans.

Case Study: USA

The Transamerica Pyramid in San Francisco was built to withstand earthquakes. When a magnitude 7.1 earthquake struck California in 1989 the top floors swayed more than 30 cm from side to side but the building was not damaged. No one was seriously injured.

A

Case Study: India

In rich *and* poor parts of the world, buildings are tested for their ability to survive earthquakes. In India, different types of houses are built on a platform. Then a tractor shakes the platform to see which building stands up best in an earthquake.

B

Case Study: Peru

In Peru many people are poor, so the government has trained people to build simple and cheap earthquake-proof buildings. In **C**, the roof is made from timber and thatch. The walls are made from bamboo, covered with mud. These materials are flexible and can be found locally.

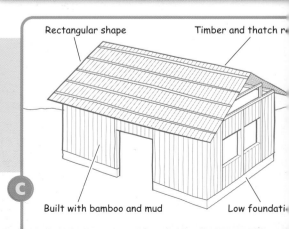

Rectangular shape   Timber and thatch r

Built with bamboo and mud   Low foundati

C

Case Study: West Coast, USA
Preparing an earthquake plan

> Choose a safe place in every room – under a table or against an inside wall where nothing can fall on you.
>
> Practise DROP, COVER, AND HOLD ON at least twice a year. Drop under a table, hold on, and protect your eyes.
>
> Find out ways you can protect your home, such as bolting the house to its foundation.
>
> Take a first-aid class.
>
> Train in how to use a fire extinguisher.
>
> Bolt bookcases, china cabinets and other tall furniture to the wall. Put strong latches on cupboards. Strap the water heater to the wall.
>
> Prepare a Disaster Kit for the home and car containing:
>
> – first-aid kit
>
> – canned food and can-opener
>
> – fifteen litres of water per person
>
> – protective clothing and sleeping-bags
>
> – radio, flashlight and batteries
>
> – written instructions for how to turn off gas, electricity and water.

D

Rich *and* poor countries carry out earthquake drills. These Californian schoolchildren are practising an earthquake drill.

F

Monitoring how structures behave

Scientists have put instruments into dams, bridges, pipelines, roads and buildings to monitor how they behave during earthquakes. This man is checking earthquake monitoring equipment in California.

E

Activities

1. Locate the countries in each of the case studies (**A**, **B**, **C** and **D**) on an outline world map.

2. The different ways of reducing the effects of earthquakes can be classified according to whether they involve:

   - educating people about what to do before, during or after an earthquake
   - improving buildings through better design and construction
   - monitoring earth movements.

   Shade the annotation boxes in three different colours according to which classification they match. Some boxes may require more than one colour.

3. Add a key and a title to your map.

How can aid help the victims of earthquakes and volcanoes?

One way of helping countries that have been affected by earthquakes or volcanic eruptions is to give them **aid**. Aid is another word for 'help'. Aid can be given in many different forms. Some of these are shown in **A**.

There are two main types of aid:

- ⊚ **Official aid:** this is given by a government.

- ⊚ **Voluntary aid:** this is provided by charities such as Oxfam, the Red Cross and Christian Aid.

Aid can be given in two ways:

- ⊚ **Short-term emergency relief aid:** this is used to save lives. It helps with immediate problems caused by events such as earthquakes, volcanic eruptions, floods and wars.

- ⊚ **Long-term development aid:** this makes people's living standards better by improving things like food production, health care and water supply. Long-term aid means that poorer countries can help themselves in the future.

Money to pay for supplies or rebuilding programmes, e.g. housing, roads, energy

Technology, e.g. heat-seeking equipment or computers to help manage the relief operations

Different forms of aid

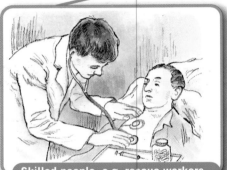
Skilled people, e.g. rescue workers, doctors and engineers, who can give advice and help people

Relief supplies: food, clothing, clean water, tents, planes and medical equipment

Activities

① Look up each charity in the list below on the Internet. For each one:

  a Write down its full name.

  b Name the countries where the charity is providing aid at the moment.

  c Say whether it provides short-term aid. If so, list the types of disasters involved.

    www.care.org.uk   www.cafod.org.uk   www.christian-aid.org.uk

    www.unicef.org.uk   www.netaid.org   www.oxfam.org.uk

    www.redcross.org.uk   www.doctorswithoutborders.org

② Make a list of the different sorts of aid that the charities provide.

B An American relief team's equipment arrives in Turkey

| Toilet and shower porta-cabins with septic tanks | Emergency health kits with a shelf life of five years | Rescue teams with sniffer dogs |

| Counselling emotionally stressed children | Short-term emergency relief aid | AID TO TURKEY | Long-term development aid | Food parcels |

| Measles vaccinations | Tents and blankets | Teams of doctors and nurses | Body-heat sensors | Education and play kits for schools |

C Different forms of aid that were donated to Turkey following the earthquake in August 1999

Activities

3
a Make a copy of **C**. Use a whole page and space out the boxes.

b Draw an arrow from each example of aid in the pink boxes to either the short-term or the long-term aid box.

c If you think the example may be both short-term and long-term, draw an arrow to both blue boxes. Three have been done for you.

4 Compare your answers with one other person. Where you disagree, discuss the reasons for this.

Case Study

How has UNICEF provided aid for victims of the 1999 Turkish earthquakes?

UNICEF (United Nations Children's Fund) is a charity that supports children and helps to meet their basic needs. It aims to provide children with health care and food, clean water and education. Seven months after the Izmit earthquake of August 1999 over 77 000 children under 8 were still homeless. Table **D** shows who donated money to UNICEF's long-term 'Recovery Plan for Turkish Children'. Table **E** shows you how the money was spent.

Groups that donated money	Amount donated (millions of US dollars)
Governments	7
UNICEF Committees	7.5
Total	14.5

D Money donated to UNICEF for the Turkish Recovery Plan

What money was spent on	Amount spent (millions of US dollars)
Water and sanitation	5
Education	4
Health	3
Emotional counselling	2.3
Transport	0.1
Children's play areas	0.1
Total	14.5

E How UNICEF spent aid money for the Recovery Plan

Adapted from: *UNICEF Recovery Plan for Turkish Children*, 13 March 2000

Activities

5 Copy and finish the two different types of graph to show the information on tables **D** and **E**. (1)(2)(3)

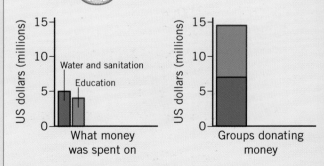

6 In what ways do your graphs show the information more clearly than the tables?

7 Which graph do you think shows the information best? Give reasons for your answer.

8
a What is meant by 'water and sanitation'?

b Why do you think that UNICEF spent most money on this?

Why do people choose to live in active zones?

A Geothermal energy (heat from the Earth) can be used to generate electrical power. This power station in Iceland also supplies the hot spring water for the local spa resort. Geothermal heat warms more than 70 per cent of homes in Iceland.

C This grid of fields is near Mount Aso in Japan. Over thousands of years, volcanic rocks have broken down to form some of the most fertile soils on Earth.

B Tourists are attracted to active zones to sightsee and to take part in activities. Here, in Lanzarote, tourists watch as a branch is set alight by the heat of the volcanic crater.

D My family has lived on the slopes of Mount Etna for many generations. We are prepared to live with the danger because we love it here ... it is our home.

Activities

1 **a** Draw a table like the one below.

    b Fill in some disadvantages and advantages.

Disadvantages of living in an active zone	Advantages of living in an active zone
Earthquakes could destroy your home	Cheap electricity from geothermal energy

2 Look at the two lists you have written.

    a Are there more advantages or more disadvantages?

    b Which are more important, the advantages or the disadvantages? Explain why you think this is.

Review and reflect

Key enquiry questions	Page numbers	Case Studies	What I learned about or did
What do you already know about earthquakes and volcanoes?	20, 21		Cause and effect
Where do volcanoes and earthquakes occur?	22, 23		Located features on a map
Why do volcanoes and earthquakes occur where they do?	24		Compared patterns on two maps
What are volcanoes?	25		Created a wordscape
What happens when a volcano erupts?	26, 27, 28, 29	Mount Pinatubo, Philippines	Annotated a map and cross-section
What happens in an earthquake?	30, 31		Researched using the Internet
How do earthquakes affect people and places?	32, 33		Explained how earthquakes affect people's lives
How do people feel after an earthquake?	33		Wrote a poem on the feelings of an earthquake victim
What happened in the 1999 earthquake in Turkey?	34, 35, 36, 37	Izmit, Turkey	Researched an enquiry question
How can people make earthquakes less of a hazard?	38, 39		Described and explained
How can aid help the victims of earthquakes and volcanoes?	40, 41		Classified information
Why do people choose to live in active zones?	42		How to weigh up advantages and disadvantages

Activities

1. Make a large copy of the table above. For each enquiry question, look back at your work for this unit and write down the names of the places you have studied in the 'Case Studies' column. Some have already been done to help you.

2. Write down the three most important things you have learned from your work on the Restless Earth. Explain why you chose them.

3. Write down three things you did or learned that might be useful in other subject areas. For example, writing a report would be useful in a history lesson.

4. Write down which activities you found most difficult. Give reasons for your choices.

help!

These ideas may help you to answer question 3.

- Classification
- Research
- Writing in report genre
- Writing in recount genre
- Asking geographical questions
- Using an atlas
- Drawing graphs
- Working with others.

3 People everywhere

Learn about

The rapid increase in the population of Planet Earth is an issue that your generation will have to face. It has great consequences for large numbers of people around the world now. In this unit you will learn about:

- what has happened to the world's population over the past 200 years
- why the population is increasing so rapidly
- what geographers mean by population density
- why some parts of the world are more crowded than others
- what geographers mean by 'settlement'
- the kind of sites which encourage settlements to grow
- the problems that occur when settlements grow very large.

World Population

Planet Earth, population 6 billion

Action needed now to avert disaster

Every day the world gains another 230 000 people – gains equal to a city the size of Sunderland. Every week there is another Birmingham, every month another London and every year another Germany. All these new people will need food, water and shelter.

97% of population growth will be in the developing world. Many people in LEDCs are poor.

Good news

Population growth has slowed down in richer countries

Bad news

40% of the world's population is under 15 years of age. Soon these children will be parents themselves, so the population is set to grow more.

People are now more healthy and live longer, which is good! The problem is that each person needs more of the world's resources.

About 75 million pregnancies each year are unwanted. Many women want better birth control and family planning services.

In some ways, reaching 6 billion people is a triumph; it means that people are healthier and are living longer. People are not problems in themselves, but what they consume and how they share the Earth's resources could lead to very great problems that cannot be ignored.

A

Activities

1 Make a larger copy of the graph below. Use Table **B** to show world population growth on the graph. Give your graph a title. (1)(2)(3)

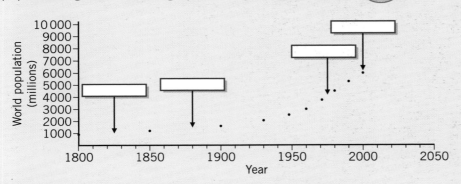

2 From your graph, estimate the population in 2050.

3 Now add these labels to your graph. Take care to put each one with the correct arrow.

- ◎ Population reaches 1000 million
- ◎ Slow population growth
- ◎ Steep population growth
- ◎ Six billion people in the world

4 Write a paragraph to summarise what the graph tells you about world population growth since 1800. Use the sentences below to get started.

- ◎ In 1800 there were less than _____ million people in the world.
- ◎ During the 1800s...
- ◎ Then in the 1900s population growth...
- ◎ Now...
- ◎ In future...

5 Read the facts in **A**. Why is population growth such a problem? Choose two facts that show the problem.

6 Will things get better or worse in future? Explain your answer carefully.

7 **Extension**

Look up http://www.y6b.org/ to find out more about the world's population. Select information to add to your answers to questions **1** to **5**. (ICT)

The 6 billion milestone

On Tuesday 12 October 1999 the world's population was estimated to have reached 6 billion people. It took until 1804 for the population of our planet to reach 1 billion (that is, 1000 million) people, yet it took only 12 years for the population to increase from 5 billion to 6 billion.

Year	World population (millions)
1800	900
1850	1200
1900	1600
1930	2000
1950	2500
1960	3000
1970	3700
1980	4500
1990	5300
2000	6000

B How the world's population has changed since 1800

Why is the population of the world going up so much?

To understand this, you have to think of the population of a country as a system, like a set of scales. You have inputs (births) and outputs (deaths). If the inputs equal the outputs then the scales are nicely balanced (see **A**).

What happens if there are more births than deaths? To see why population growth rate is fast in some places and slow in others, you are going to look at two very different countries, Mali and the UK. Mali is a less economically developed country (**LEDC**). The UK is a more economically developed country (**MEDC**). Look at table **B** which shows some basic differences.

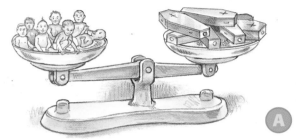

A

Country	UK	Mali
Birth rate	13	50
Death rate	11	20
Annual growth rate		
Infant mortality rate	6	134
Life expectancy (male / female)	74 / 79	44 / 48

B Population facts for UK and Mali

Activities

1 Copy out table **B**. Work out the figures for the annual growth rate (see Getting Technical) and add them to your table. (1 2 3)

2 Copy and complete this paragraph by choosing the correct words from the pairs. The UK has quite a <u>low/high</u> birth rate and a <u>low/high</u> death rate. In Mali the birth rate is very <u>similar/different</u> from the death rate, because it is much higher. This means that Mali's growth rate is much <u>higher/lower</u> than the UK's. In the UK people can expect to live <u>longer/shorter</u> lives than in Mali, but in both countries men/women live longer. In <u>the UK/Mali</u> the infant mortality rate is very high.

3 In pairs, choose one of the 'heads' below. Then choose one of the 'tails'. Write out the head and the tail, and then work out the result that goes with them. The first one has been done for you. Suggest as many heads and tails for each result as you can.

Heads	Tails	Results
High birth rate	High death rate	Population grows fast
Medium birth rate	Medium death rate	Population grows slowly
Low birth rate	Low death rate	Population stable
		Population goes down

High birth rate + Low death rate → Population grows fast

Getting Technical ▼

◎ **Birth rate**
The **birth rate** of a country is the average number of babies born to every 1000 people each year.

◎ **Death rate**
The **death rate** of a country is the average number of people who die for every 1000 people each year.

◎ **Annual growth rate**
Annual growth rate is found by taking away the death rate from the birth rate. It tells you how many extra people there are in a country per thousand each year. If the growth rate is large, the population is growing a lot. If it is a negative number, the population is actually going down each year. A country has a **stable population** when the death rate and birth rate are the same.

◎ **Infant mortality rate**
Infant mortality rate is a special type of death rate. It is the number of babies who die before their first birthday for every 1000 babies born.

◎ **Life expectancy**
Life expectancy is the average number of years that a person might expect to live. It gives a clue about the general health of a country's population.

◎ **Migration**
The population will change if people move either into or out of a country. When people move into a country it is called **immigration**. When people move out of a country it is called **emigration**.

Death rates have been going down all over the world

Death rates generally have been falling in most parts of the world over the past hundred years. There are a number of reasons for this.

Illnesses have been prevented because:

⚬ more people have access to clean water

⚬ more people enjoy a varied **diet**, which means better health

⚬ more babies are born in hospital, where expert help is on hand, rather than at home, especially in richer countries

⚬ more children are **inoculated** against killer diseases such as polio.

More ill people can be cured because of:

⚬ better health facilities, such as clinics and hospitals

⚬ better knowledge of disease.

Education and changes to our surroundings have helped as well, including:

⚬ better health education

⚬ better living conditions for some people

⚬ more women in LEDCs receiving education

⚬ in MEDCs, improved design for new housing and strict building regulations.

C Clean water helps people to stay healthy

Activities

❶ Choose the one **factor** (reason) that you feel has been the most important in bringing down death rates. Discuss this with a partner. Give reasons for your choice.

❷ Put the rest of the reasons in order of importance.

❸ Start to make a word bank of key words for this unit.

   a Start with the words in **bold** on this page.

   b Add any key words you have learned from pages 44–46.

Birth rates are getting lower but are more difficult to reduce

Photographs **D** and **E** show two families in very different parts of the world. Why are familiies usually so much larger in poor countries? There are lots of reasons.

The role of children in MEDCs like the UK

In the UK, bringing up children is expensive for parents. Feeding, clothing and educating a child will cost, on average, more than £50 000 by the time he or she is 17. Children can be seen as an **economic burden** to their parents.

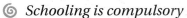
D A small family in the UK

Marcus and Cynthia Wright live in a small village in West Yorkshire, England. They both have professional jobs which take up a good deal of time. Marcus is a dentist and Cynthia is a barrister. Cynthia took maternity leave when she was 32 to have her first child, Jamie. Two years later Susie was born. Both parents juggle their time to manage their jobs and get the children to and from school and child-minders, as well as music, swimming and dancing lessons.

Schooling is compulsory

Nearly all young people go to school, and they cannot work full time until they are 16. Many young people also go to university.

Jobs are specialised

Many people want to have a career before they start a family, so parents are often quite old in the UK.

Old people get pensions

A well-developed system of pensions and benefits means that most old people can look after themselves. They don't need lots of children to provide money for them when they are old.

You don't have to get pregnant!

Family planning is available in MEDCs, so couples can choose whether or not they want to have children.

They can also choose when to start a family, so many parents wait until they have saved some money. Women in the UK have an average of only 1.7 children.

The role of children in LEDCs like Mali

In Mali most children contribute to the family income, so they are an **economic asset** to their parents. They might collect water and firewood, or help on the farm. These jobs take many hours and allow adults to do other tasks.

There are not many schools

In Mali there are very few secondary schools, and only 31% of children go to primary schools.

Old people rely on their children

Many older people rely upon their children to look after them – children are seen as a form of security when there is no state pension.

Many babies die in their first year

Infant mortality rates are high, so parents have many children to make sure that at least some of them survive.

In Mali the average family size is 6.7 children.

Fanta and Samba Coulibali live in Tomora, Mali, with their four children. A nephew also lives with them. They grow millet and struggle to find enough to eat every year. Even if the rains are good, their two small fields only give enough food for six months. This means that the family have to split up during part of the year to find food. Fanta often goes to the River Niger flood plain to help harvest rice. When they run out of food, they have to borrow sacks of millet, on which they have to pay interest.

 **A large family in Mali**

Activities

❶ Read about the roles of children in the UK and Mali. Make a copy of the grid below. Fill in the gaps. Try to include facts and figures.

	UK	Mali
Family size		The average family size is _____
Education		
Health care and family planning	Parents plan when to start a family, and children are born in hospital	
Children's work	Children do not start full-time work until they are _____	
Benefits	Elderly people can claim pensions	

❷ Give one reason why you think that the Wrights only have two children.

❸ Give three reasons why Fanta and Samba Coulibali want to have lots of children.

❹ The Wrights have two children and the Coulibalis have four, but which family puts most stress on the Earth's resources? Think carefully and give three reasons for your choice.

❺ How typical a UK family do you think the Wrights are? How typical are the Coulibalis? Discuss these questions with a partner, then describe what extra information you would need to find the answers.

It's not just a numbers game!

A Extended family group from one of the richest countries in the world

Population is not just about numbers of people. Geographers also ask other questions about a country's population. Some good questions are:

- What age groups make up the population of the country?
- In which parts of the country do most people live?
- How long are people expected to live?
- How many people die each year?
- How many people are born each year?

Governments and planners need to ask these questions so that they can plan things for the country. Here are some services that they need to plan.

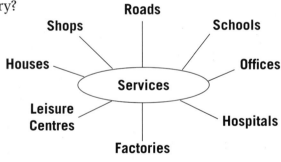

B Spider diagram of services

Activities

1 Why do planners need to ask questions? Copy and complete the table below. Work out which questions match the services.

Question	Services that need planning
How many people are born each year?	So planners can build new schools for the children.
How long are people expected to live?	
	So there are leisure facilities for all ages.
	So planners have factories in the right places.

2 What would happen if planners did not know about the population? Give two problems that might happen. Explain why.

What age groups make up the population of a country?

This is called the **population structure** of a country. It is usually shown by a **population pyramid**. Population pyramids are drawn with young children at the bottom of the pyramid and old people at the top. In most countries there are fewer old people than children, so the diagrams are usually triangular in shape. You can see population pyramids for Mali and the United Kingdom in **C** and **D**.

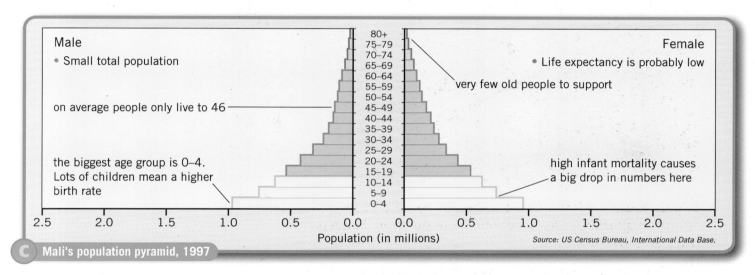

Male
- Small total population

on average people only live to 46

the biggest age group is 0–4. Lots of children mean a higher birth rate

very few old people to support

Female
- Life expectancy is probably low

high infant mortality causes a big drop in numbers here

Population (in millions)

Source: US Census Bureau, International Data Base.

C Mali's population pyramid, 1997

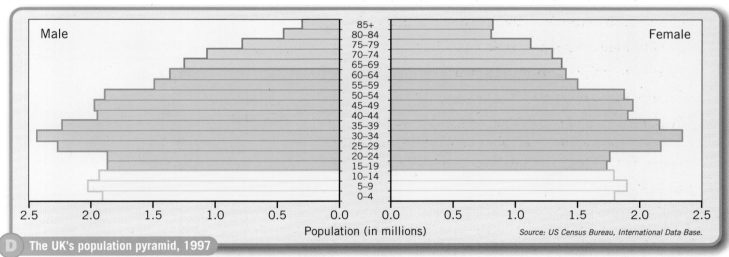

Male

Female

Population (in millions)

Source: US Census Bureau, International Data Base.

D The UK's population pyramid, 1997

Activities

1. Trace or copy **D**, the population pyramid for the UK. Add your own labels to it, like the ones for Mali. Here are some suggestions, but do add some of your own as well.

   ⊚ Compared with the older age groups in the UK the base of the pyramid is small. This shows that the UK has a low birth rate.

   ⊚ School children

   ⊚ Elderly people. This shows that … .

   ⊚ People who need jobs

Population density

Population density is a measure of how many people live in an area of land. This is counted in people for each square kilometre (km^2). If lots of people live in a small space, then there is a **high population density**. In cities, population densities can be very high: Hong Kong has a density of more than 5000 people per km^2.

A Hong Kong has a high population density

The population density of a whole country is never as high as that, because people are usually more spread out across the country. Any country with a population density of more than 100 people per km^2 is said to have a high population density. The UK has a density of 244 people per km^2.

Areas where few people live per square kilometre have a *low population density* or are described as **sparsely populated**. Mali has a population density of 8 people per km^2. This is a sparsely populated country, even though there is a high rate of population growth.

There are a number of reasons or factors why some areas are more densely populated than others. Look back at the photograph of the Himalayas on page 44. It is not difficult to see why the population is sparse. A city like Rio de Janeiro (see page 70) has a very high population density, and it is easy to see why many people decided to live there.

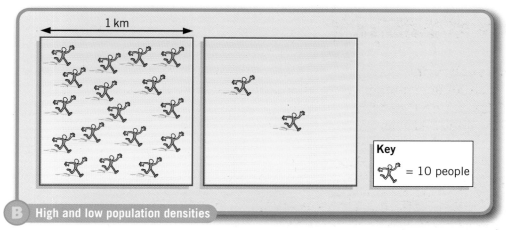

B High and low population densities

C Factors which encourage high or low population density

volcanic areas

good roads

steep slopes

foggy places

earthquake zones

high areas

lack of jobs

rich soil

rocky places

wet areas

thickly forested areas

good farming

very hot places

very cold places

temperate places

places likely to have blizzards

places with poor TV reception

coal-fields

coastal areas

river valleys

dry areas

difficult communications

industrial places

places likely to flood

sunny places

cloudy places

lowland areas

flat areas

places with many jobs

Activities

1 **a** Look at the boxes in **B**. Each one represents a square kilometre. Calculate the population density for each one.

   b Sketch copies of the boxes. Label them correctly using these words: **sparsely populated   high population density low population density.**

2 **a** Look at the photo on page 44. It is an area of low population density. Make a copy of the spider diagram below. Choose six more factors from box **C** that explain why few people live there.

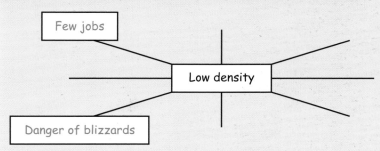

   b Draw a spider diagram for **high density** population. Label it with six factors from box **C**.

   c On the two spider diagrams you have drawn, work out which of your labels are **human factors** (to do with people). Colour these red. Then work out which of your labels are **physical factors** (natural). Colour these green.

3 Think about the place that you live.

   a Does it have a high, medium or low population density?

   b Can you give three reasons to explain why? Box **C** might help.

4 **Extension**

     ◎ Try to split the physical and human factors on your diagrams into smaller categories (climate, relief, soils, vegetation, economic, social, etc.). Use a colour key to indicate these.

     ◎ Find the places mentioned on pages 46–52 on a population density map in your atlas. How are high and low density areas shown on the map?

Case Study

Population distribution: Where do people live in Mali?

Geographers often ask these questions about the population in a country:

- Where in the country do most people live?

- Why do people live in these areas of high population density?

- Why are some areas more sparsely populated?

You have already seen that the population of Mali is increasing very rapidly (page 46). This is because of the high birth rate and the much lower death rate. In the fourteenth century, Mali had a rich and powerful empire, but today it is one of the poorest countries in the world.

Much of Mali is in the Sahara desert. The desert has grown since the 1970s, and this has put more stress on the land. Most of the farmland is near the River Niger where the soil is fertile, but mosquitoes breed in swampy areas.

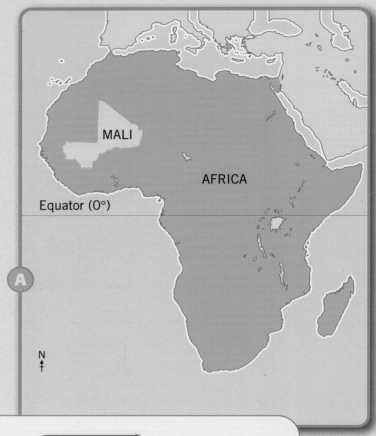

Mali fact file

Land

- Land area is 124090 km^2.
- Sixty-five per cent is desert or semi-desert.
- The land north of 15 °N is true desert.
- In the south the land is over 1000 m above sea level.

People

- Total population is 9.9 million.
- Eighty per cent of the population work in farming or fishing.
- Ten per cent of the population are nomads who follow seasonal rains to find grass for their cattle.

Trade

- Mali is a land-locked country that relies on trade with the outside world.
- Cotton is an important export crop.
- Gold-mining has increased recently and gold could be a valuable export.

Activities

1. **a** Sketch or trace the map of Mali (**B**).

    b Read the information about Mali and look at photos **C** and **D**. Add these labels to your map in the correct places.

    **Desert   Low rainfall   Higher rainfall
    Fertile farmland   Higher land**

2. Which of these statements is true?

    - There is a low population density in the north of Mali.

    - Most people live near the main rivers.

    - The driest areas have higher population density.

    a Copy the two correct statements.

    b Change one word in the false statement to make it true, then copy it out.

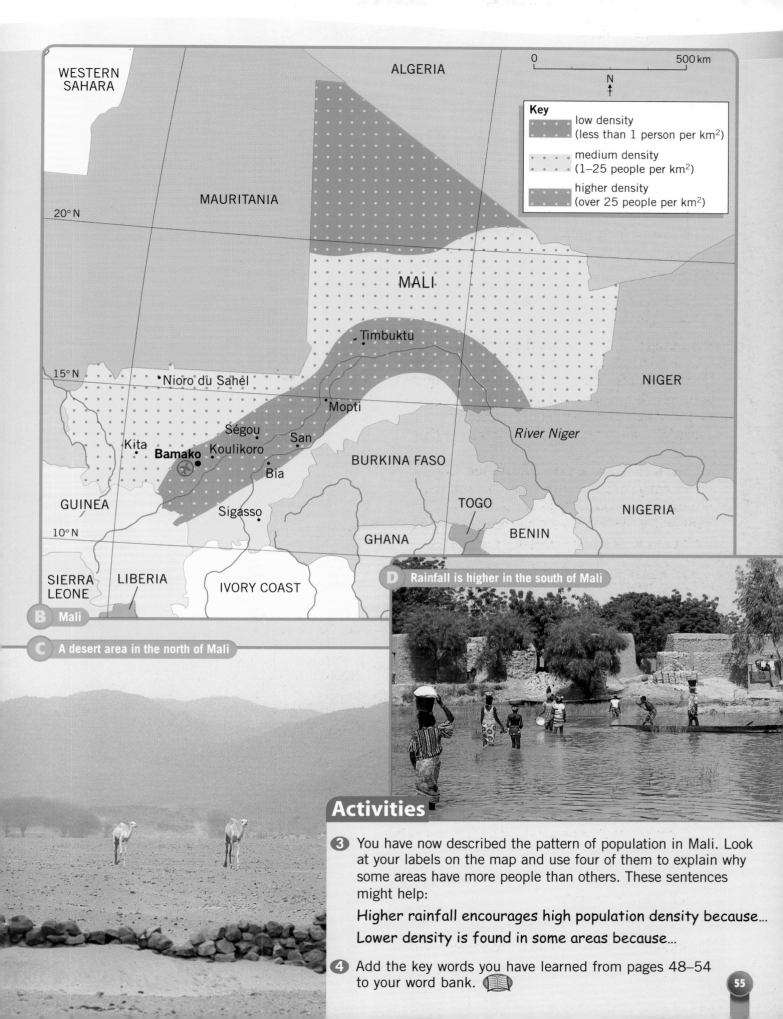

WESTERN
SAHARA

ALGERIA

0   500 km

N

Key
low density
(less than 1 person per km²)

medium density
(1–25 people per km²)

higher density
(over 25 people per km²)

MAURITANIA

20° N

MALI

•Timbuktu

15° N

•Nioro du Sahel

NIGER

•Mopti

Ségou
Kita   •   • San
•   Koulikoro
Bamako •

River Niger

•Bia

BURKINA FASO

GUINEA

TOGO

NIGERIA

10° N

Sigasso
•

BENIN

GHANA

SIERRA
LEONE

LIBERIA

IVORY COAST

D Rainfall is higher in the south of Mali

B Mali

C A desert area in the north of Mali

Activities

3 You have now described the pattern of population in Mali. Look at your labels on the map and use four of them to explain why some areas have more people than others. These sentences might help:

Higher rainfall encourages high population density because…

Lower density is found in some areas because…

4 Add the key words you have learned from pages 48–54 to your word bank.

Distribution of population: looking globally

Study map **A** closely, taking time to look at the population density in each of the seven continents throughout the world. The density of some continents is easy to describe and give reasons for. For example, Antarctica is the only continent with no permanent population. It is easy to explain why this is so (see page 53 if you need help on this). The pattern in other continents is more complicated. The pictures on this page and pages 44, 52 and 55 show some of the reasons why some parts of the world are sparsely populated and others have high population densities.

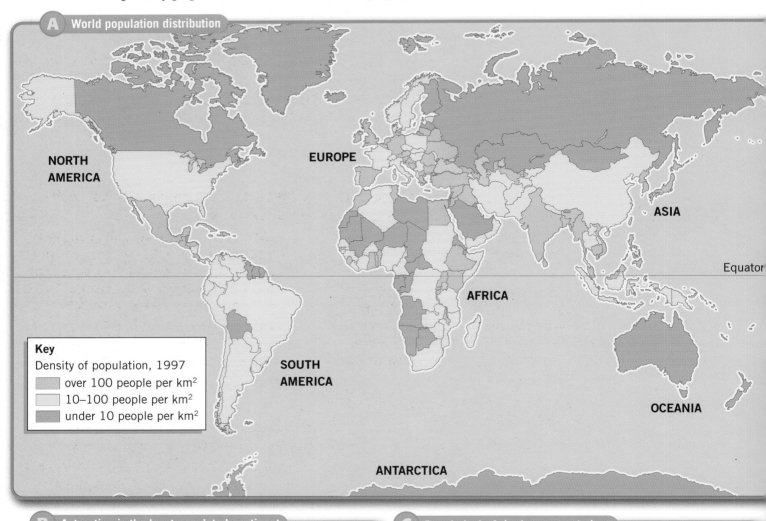

A World population distribution

NORTH AMERICA

EUROPE

ASIA

AFRICA

Equator

SOUTH AMERICA

OCEANIA

ANTARCTICA

Key
Density of population, 1997
- over 100 people per km²
- 10–100 people per km²
- under 10 people per km²

B Antarctica is the least populated continent

C Bangladesh, Asia, has a population density of about 950 people per km²

E The Nevada desert, in the United States, is sparsely populated

D Sydney, Australia, has a high population density, although overall Australia has a population of less than 10 people per km²

Fact file

Population record-breakers

- ⊚ The world's fastest growing countries are Kuwait, Namibia, Afghanistan, Mali and Tanzania.
- ⊚ The world's slowest growing countries are Belgium, Hungary, Grenada, Germany and Tonga.
- ⊚ Greenland has only 0.2 people per km².
- ⊚ Tristan da Cunha and the Pitcairn Islands have the smallest populations.
- ⊚ Macau has a population density of over 22 000 people per km².
- ⊚ The two countries with the largest populations are China and India.

Review and reflect

In this unit you have learned about population distribution and growth. Your final assignment is to produce a poster summarising what you have learned about population. Use the steps below to help you focus your ideas. Your teacher may ask you to work in a group for this assignment.

1 First, look at an atlas map showing world population distribution. On an outline map, label three parts of the world that have **high population** density and three that have **low population density**. For each place where the population density is sparse, give a reason why few people live there. Photos **D** and **E** might help.

2 Label two countries where the population is growing fast and two countries where it is growing slowly.

3 Here are two population pyramids.

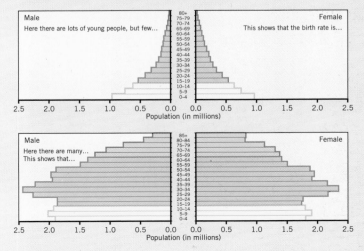

Add these to your poster and complete the labels next to each pyramid.

4 Finally, discuss why population growth might be a problem in the future. How can the problem be solved? Look at the ideas in box **F** and organize them into two columns in a copy of the table below.

Ways to slow population growth	Ways to make sure there are enough resources

Why are some ideas difficult to organize? Choose the three best ways to solve the population problem and explain how each idea would help. Add this work to your poster, but think carefully where to put each idea.

- ⊚ More birth control for parents who want it
- ⊚ Use less fossil fuel
- ⊚ Recycle more materials
- ⊚ Better health care for children
- ⊚ More benefits and pensions for old people
- ⊚ Irrigate deserts with water supply
- ⊚ Don't waste resources
- ⊚ Educate people

F Ways of lessening the population crisis

What is a settlement?

A settlement is a place where people live. Geographers are often interested in how many people live within a particular area (*settlement size* or *type*), the exact location of the settlement (*settlement site*) and what goes on in the settlement (*settlement function*).

You are going to look at the answers to these three enquiry questions:

- What is a settlement?
- Where do people build settlements?
- Why do they choose those places to build settlements?

Where do you live?

Most people, if asked this very basic question, would reply that they lived in a house. Some people might name the place or the road. Most people live in one place throughout the year, and are said to live in a **permanent settlement**. A few people might have difficulty in giving a straightforward answer: they may live in a **temporary settlement** and move from place to place.

Activities

1. Which of these photos (**A–G**) show a settlement?

2. Why are the other photos *not* settlements? Give reasons.

Activities

3 Here are some settlements arranged into two types, 'permanent' and 'temporary'. Copy the diagram and add some more settlements of your own. Could some be both?

Permanent settlements	Temporary settlements
Village	Refugee camp
Hamlet	Squatter settlement

4 Why do some people live in temporary settlements? Construct a brainstorm diagram to show all your ideas. If people are *forced* to live in a temporary settlement, colour the reason red. Use blue to show the reasons why people *choose* to do so.

5 **Extension**

Research and collect more pictures that show settlements in different places. For each picture, write one thing that it shows. Here are some ideas:

<u>Materials</u>: Houses here are made from _____ because...

<u>Shape</u>: This settlement is in a long line because...

<u>Permanence</u>: This settlement is temporary because...

Settlement sites

The exact position that a settlement occupies is often called its **site**. Many settlements have very useful sites that have encouraged the settlements to grow. Look at these **factors** that make good settlement sites.

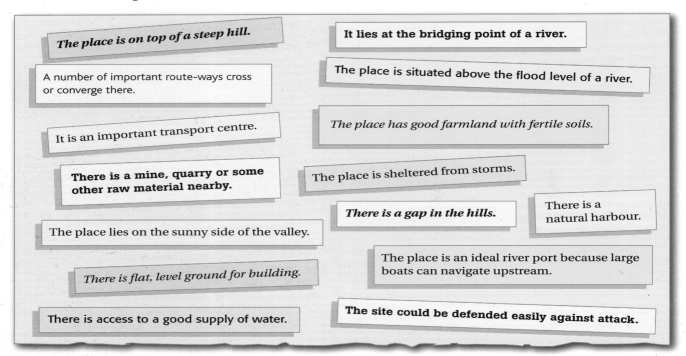

The place is on top of a steep hill.

A number of important route-ways cross or converge there.

It is an important transport centre.

There is a mine, quarry or some other raw material nearby.

The place lies on the sunny side of the valley.

There is flat, level ground for building.

There is access to a good supply of water.

It lies at the bridging point of a river.

The place is situated above the flood level of a river.

The place has good farmland with fertile soils.

The place is sheltered from storms.

There is a gap in the hills.

There is a natural harbour.

The place is an ideal river port because large boats can navigate upstream.

The site could be defended easily against attack.

Activities

① Each of the factors above makes you think 'so what?' Choose three of the factors and answer the 'so what' question, like this:

| There is access to a good supply of water. | → | **So what?** | → | So, in the past before pipelines, it was easy for people to get drinking water. |

② How many of the factors are **physical**? Can you say why physical factors were important reasons for settlement sites?

③ Some settlements stop growing or even disappear. Can you do some 'so what?' answers for the examples on the right?

There is not much flat land.

There is flooding from a river or the sea.

A volcano erupts.

The local factory closes.

Important roads no longer pass through the town.

The surrounding area is very hilly.

Local resources run out.

The site of a settlement is not necessarily good; this may mean that the settlement does not grow as fast as those with more successful sites. Here are some examples of sites that are not very good.

⑥ There is little flat land.

⑥ The settlement can't expand because of a major road.

⑥ The roads have become very congested because they are too narrow.

⑥ There is flooding from a river or the sea.

⑥ Important roads no longer pass through the settlement.

⑥ The original reason for its existence has now gone.

Settlement along the River Severn

The River Severn is the UK's longest river. It flows from Wales through parts of England and runs into the Bristol Channel. Until the railways were built in the mid 1800s, it was much easier to carry people and goods by boat than over the land, so many people settled near rivers like the Severn. Look carefully at the map on this page. It shows the course of the river and the sites of many settlements along it. Then look at the information about some of these sites on pages 62–66 before you do the activity on page 67.

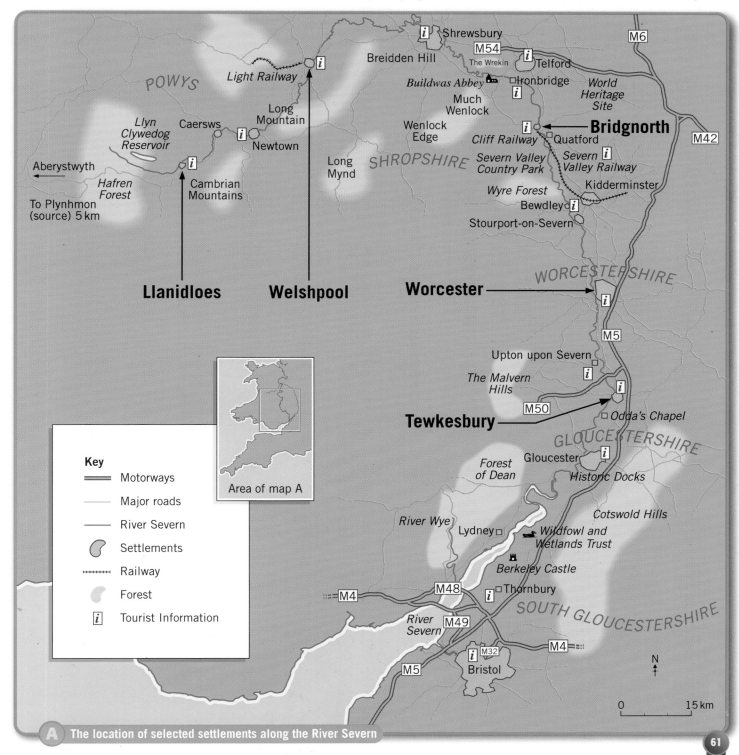

Key
- ▬▬ Motorways
- ─── Major roads
- ─── River Severn
- Settlements
- ┅┅┅ Railway
- Forest
- *i* Tourist Information

Area of map A

A The location of selected settlements along the River Severn

Tewkesbury

Tewkesbury has a long street which is lined with ancient buildings, including the Abbey. It is sited on the eastern side of the River Severn at its **confluence** (joining place) with the River Avon.

B Aerial view of Tewkesbury

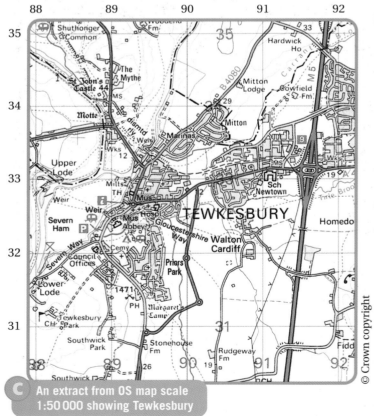

© Crown copyright

C An extract from OS map scale 1:50 000 showing Tewkesbury

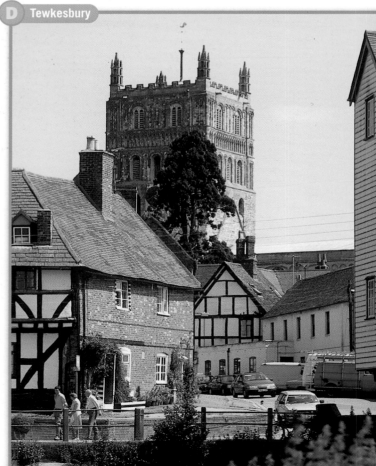

D Tewkesbury

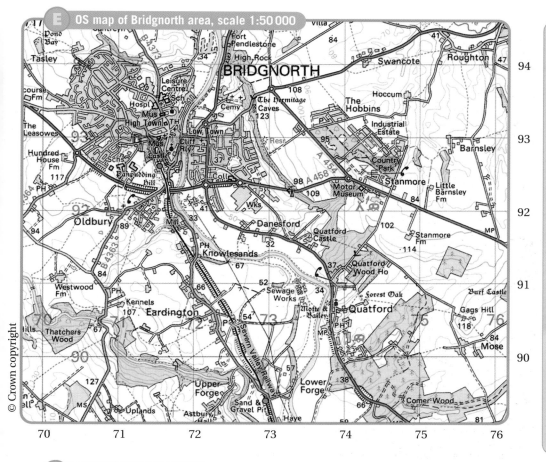

E OS map of Bridgnorth area, scale 1:50 000

© Crown copyright

Bridgnorth

The lower part of the town, or Low Town, lies either side of the magnificent River Severn, while the higher part, or High Town, is perched on dramatic sandstone cliffs 30 metres high. The two parts of the town are linked by historic winding steps and a unique cliff railway.

There is so much to see, both in the town itself and in the surrounding area, that visitors are well advised to allow plenty of time for their visit to this ancient market town!

F Aerial view of Bridgnorth

Llanidloes

Llanidloes is a historic market town in the centre of Wales. It lies at the confluence (joining place) of the rivers Clywedog and Severn. There are two bridges over the Severn in the town. The main A470(T) bypasses the town on the south-east. The site of the town is restricted on the north and north-west by steep slopes. The Tudor market hall in the picture is now a museum. There are many other interesting buildings from Tudor, Georgian and Victorian times.

G The market hall in Llanidloes was built in Tudor times

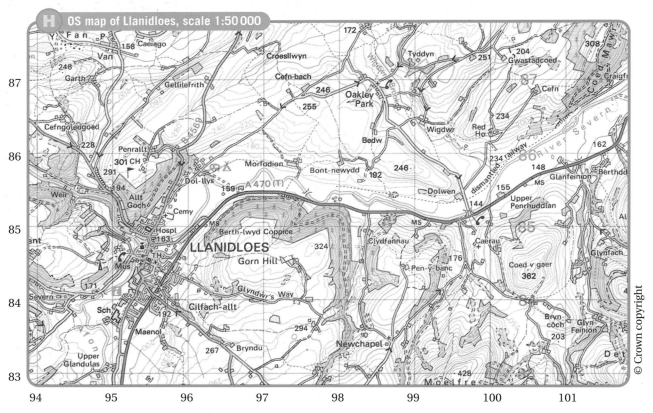

H OS map of Llanidloes, scale 1:50 000

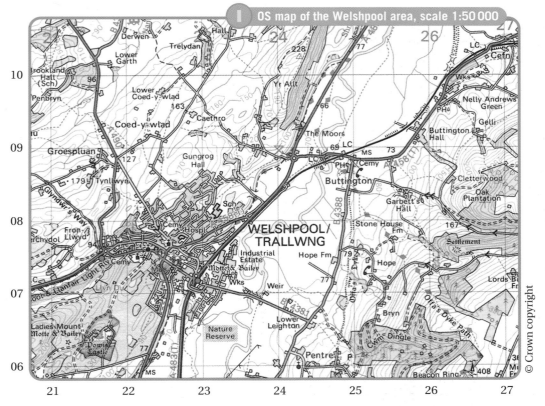

I OS map of the Welshpool area, scale 1:50 000

© Crown copyright

Welshpool

Welshpool is a busy market town in Mid Wales. Bronze Age remains have been found nearby, and it was a civilian settlement in Roman times. Medieval Powis Castle, 1.5 km south of the town, is perched on a rock with terraced gardens below.

J The main street in Welshpool attracts shoppers from the surrounding countryside

Historic Worcester

The city of Worcester is situated on the River Severn, the longest river in Britain. The original settlement was sited on the east bank of the river but today Worcester has grown into a city of 90,000 people.

The battle of Worcester in 1651, when Oliver Cromwell defeated Prince Charles, marked the end of the Civil War in England. It earned Worcester the name "The Faithful City" for its Royalist support.

Worcester is home to Royal Worcester Porcelain and the famous 'Worcester Sauce', and it is the birthplace of the British composer, Sir Edward Elgar.

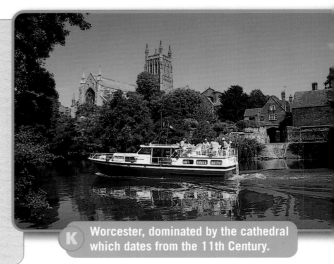

K Worcester, dominated by the cathedral which dates from the 11th Century.

L OS map of the Worcester area, scale 1:50 000

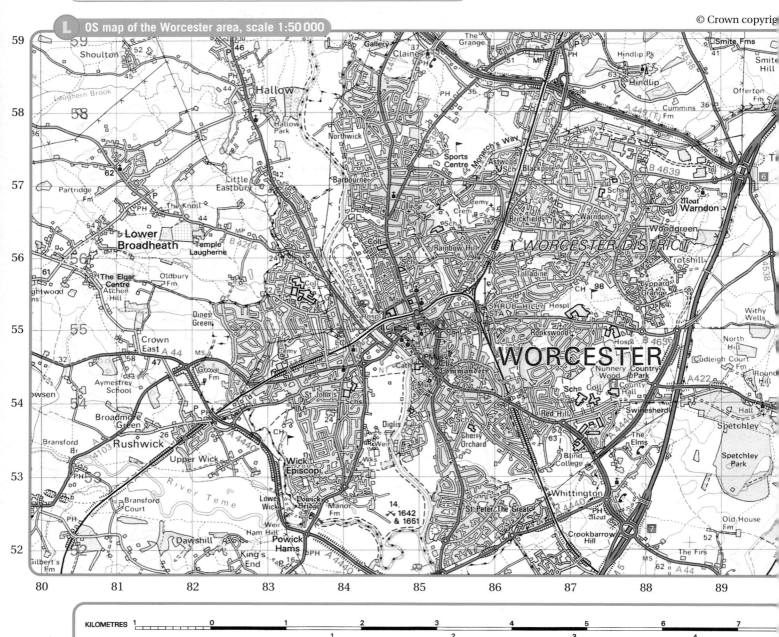

KILOMETRES

M Scale bar for 1:50 000 scale maps

Activities

1 Look back at map **A** on page 61 and the other information for the five settlements on the River Severn. For each settlement, use clues from the maps, photos and text to try to analyse its site. You might like to set your work for each settlement out like this:

Settlement name	Bridgnorth
Settlement type (city, large town, market town, village)	Market town
Location	Shropshire
Site description	Bridgnorth is sited on a steep hill.
Good things about its site	It is a good place to cross the river. High Town is safe from flooding.
Bad things about its site	Low Town might flood, and there are some steep slopes. This makes it difficult to grow and expand.
My verdict (marks out of 10 for the settlement site)	5/10
Reasons for my verdict	It was a good place when defence was important, but now …
Special features and *functions* of the settlement	• Castle • Museum • Leisure centre • Hospital

2 Use the scale to estimate the size of each settlement you have studied. Find the size of the settlement in kilometres from north to south and west to east.

3 Make a display of your work by organising your notes on each settlement around a large copy of map **A** on page 61.

4 Add words you have learned about settlement to your word bank.

5 **Extension**
Study the 1:50 000 OS map of the area where you live. Analyse the sites of four or five different settlements. How do they compare with those in the Severn Valley?

The living city

In this section, you are going to investigate a much larger settlement, Rio de Janeiro, in South America. Rio de Janeiro is a very large city in a part of the world very different from the Severn Valley. After investigating this city, you should have the skills to enquire into another city anywhere in the world. For any city, try to investigate:

- the location of the city
- what different parts of the city are like
- why there are differences between the different parts of the city
- what changes are taking place within the settlement
- how people are trying to improve the environments in which they live.

Investigating Rio de Janeiro

The first stage in this geographical investigation or **enquiry** is to make sure you understand clearly the location of this settlement. Geographers describe the location of a settlement in two ways.

The **site** of a settlement means its detailed location. When we describe the site, we look closely at the land that the settlement is built on. We need to consider:

- details of relief features – is it steep, flat or high on a hill?
- details of water – is it on a river or next to a stream or lake?
- other details – is it on good farmland, on forested land etc?

The **situation** of a settlement looks at the broader picture of what is around it. We might describe other places that are nearby. We might use distances and directions to describe the situation. Tewkesbury, for example, is in the west of England, in Gloucestershire. It is near to Wales and 15 km south of Worcester.

help!

Atlas entries are sometimes listed like this:

Wolverhampton	5	D4	52°N	2°W
place or feature	page	grid square	latitude	longitude

Activities

1. Use your atlas to locate the city of Rio de Janeiro. Look up the entry in the index of your atlas and write that down exactly.

2. Using the index entry, write a few sentences to describe how it helps you to find where the city is on one of the atlas maps. You could use your own words or set it out like this:

   > Rio de Janeiro is at latitude ____ °S and longitude ____ °W. It is found on page ____ of my atlas. It is in the grid square ____. The city is in the country of ____ …

3. a Use the index entry to find Rio de Janeiro in the atlas. Draw a quick sketch map to show its situation within the continent of South America and the country of Brazil.

   b Write two sentences which describe the situation of Rio. Label these onto your sketch map.

4. Look at the picture and the detailed map of Rio de Janeiro. Write a description of the site of the city.

Setting the scene – what is Rio like?

Rio de Janeiro is a very large city of over 11 million people. It is world famous for its natural beauty, its carnival and its samba (a dance). It is sited on a magnificent bay with the beautiful beaches of Ipanema and Copacabana on one side and steep, forest-covered mountains on the other.

Rio de Janeiro has two very famous landmarks: the Sugar Loaf Mountain, and a statue called 'Christ the Redeemer'. This statue is sited at the top of Corcovado Mountain, and can be seen for miles around. The map and photographs give some idea what the city is like.

A Rio carnival

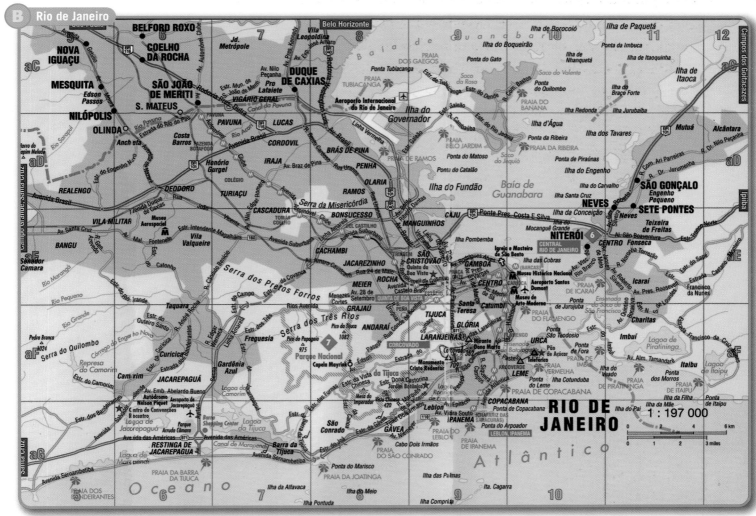

B Rio de Janeiro

C Aerial view of Rio de Janeiro

The city centre (or Downtown Rio)

Rio is a huge city with a noisy centre that is busy 24 hours a day. This Central Business District (CBD) is full of expensive shops and offices. Thousands of street traders also come here to sell their goods. Rio does not have much flat land because of its steep mountains. There is not much space in the CBD, so buildings are tall. These high-rise apartments and offices are only for rich people and businesses who can afford them. There isn't much space for roads, so tunnels are cut through the hills, and the streets are crowded and congested.

D Downtown Rio

Activities

5 Write a paragraph to describe what the centre of Rio is like. Here are some words to help you, but choose the right ones and find some others for yourself.

**noisy/quiet   spacious/congested   scruffy/smart
flat/steep   cheap/expensive   old/new**

Add some drawings, maps or cartoons to make your description more detailed.

6 Now explain why the city centre is like it is. Start with six of the words that you chose for question 5 and suggest why the city centre is like that.

help! ICT

Use ICT to add to your description of the city centre.

⊛ Start by looking at CD-ROM encyclopaedias. Remember to edit text before you use it.

⊛ Extend your investigation by searching the Internet. http://www.ipanema.com and http://www.bondinho.com.br/ may give useful results. Use a search engine to make your own enquiry.

Contrasts within the city

From a distance, Rio looks rich and smart. But many of its residents are very poor. Not far from the glamorous beaches of Copacabana and Ipanema, you can find serious crime such as drugs trafficking and violence. It is very difficult for the city authorities to keep everything under control and to provide services for everyone.

You are going to look at three different parts of the city:

- Rocinha near the CBD
- Barra to the west of Rio
- favelas on the edge of the city.

Rocinha

Rocinha is a poor area, with about 100 000 residents. It is an unplanned area called a **favela** or **shanty town**, where people have built their own houses. Rocinha is like a town within the city. It is sited on steep slopes overlooking Copacabana beach.

The first residents of this huge favela came from the Brazilian countryside 40 years ago to find a better life in the city. A city like Rio thrives on cheap **labour**. Some people work in the factories around Rio's port. Others make a living from offering services around the city, such as selling food, working in bars, cleaning for better-off families, security work or fetching and carrying goods. Many of these jobs are **informal** and may be poorly paid.

When Rocinha was a new settlement, it was made up of wooden shacks. These were often perched unsafely on the steep slopes found all over the city. Now things are different. The houses are mainly built of brick and have rooms with balconies. There are basic services such as electricity, rubbish collection, street-lighting, running water and sewage disposal. Often these services were organised by the residents themselves: they did not wait for the city authorities to act.

Despite the community spirit within the favelas, they are still tough places to live. Their crime rates are often unacceptably high. However, by doing well at school, young people can try to escape the poverty of the favelas. Vehicles cannot get into Rochina because of the steep, narrow streets, so people have to walk everywhere.

Barra da Tijuca

The new 'city' of Barra da Tijuca is 30 km to the west of Rio. There are 150 000 people living in Barra. Like Rio,

E Rocinha

F Barra da Tijuca

Barra is on the coast. Unlike Rio, there is plenty of flat land, so there is room to expand.

Many people live in high-rise apartments with high security, and there are excellent services, for example shopping malls along the dual carriageways. The beach at Barra is less crowded and more exclusive than those nearer to the city centre. Many of Rio's professional people are leaving the city to live in places on the outskirts like Barra. They can commute back on the motorway to the city centre if they need to, while enjoying the safer, quieter and more exclusive living conditions.

Favelas on the edge of Rio

There is an **out-migration** of rich people to places like Barra, but this is balanced by poor people who are still moving into Rio. Like many LEDCs, there is an **in-migration** of people from Brazil's countryside who want a better way of life. With nowhere else to live, the newest arrivals have to fend for themselves. Jobs are difficult to find, and many of them become street traders, earning very low wages. They find spare land and build their own homes. The only spaces in a city like Rio are right on the edge of the city, or in dangerous places that no one else wants (see **G**). The sites of favelas

G Favela built on Rio's steep slopes

are often on land that is very steep, or on land that will flood. People often live there illegally, because the land belongs to someone else.

Activities

7 Make a copy of the table below and use the headings to compare the three different housing areas of Rio. Try to add as much detail as possible.

	Rocinha	Barra	A new Favela
Situation	Near the city centre		
Site			On steep slopes
What type of houses are there?	Used to be wooden shacks. Now...		
What services are available?			None
What jobs do people do?			
How wealthy are the residents?	Mostly quite poor		

8 Which is the best place to live? Put these three places in rank order, and explain what makes one place better than another.

9 Choose one of the places and say how *you* think it will change in future. Explain why.

help!

Try searching the Internet for more information, as you did for the city centre. **ICT**

Activities

10 Your final task is to produce a labelled poster to summarise the contrasts in the city of Rio. You may be asked to work in a pair or a group for this activity.

a Draw a sketch map of the city. Label the city centre, Rocinha, Barra da Tijuca and the latest developments on the outskirts of Rio.

b Choose the most important parts of your answers to questions 5, 6 and 7, and add them to your map as labels, like this one:

> CBD. Mainly shops and offices with expensive apartments.

You can draw some of the buildings in the photos to illustrate the different parts of the city.

11 **Extension**

Read the tourist brochure descriptions of the towns on pages 64 and 65. Now do one for Rio de Janeiro. Remember that a tourist brochure would not want to put people off, but is trying to attract them to visit. Give lots of information, but choose your words carefully.

Review and reflect

Summary of the Rio de Janeiro investigation

	Page
Geographers often start their investigations into places by locating them. You found out the **situation** of Rio by using an atlas.	68
More detailed maps and photographs of the city showed you the **site** of the settlement, the place where it is built.	69–70
Like many towns and cities, Rio has a central area which geographers call the **central business district**.	70
Outside the centre of the city, there are great contrasts between different neighbourhoods. In cities like Rio the pressure for housing is often so great that people are forced to build their own houses.	71–72

In time, some areas of self-build housing, or **favelas**, are improved. But on the edge of the city, new arrivals have to find a home.

Activities

Look back at your work on Rio de Janeiro using the page numbers in the summary table above to help.

1 In pairs, test that you understand what the key words (in bold) mean. For each word, try to think of another place where you can describe an example.

2 Discuss what was the most interesting thing you found out, a new skill you learned and something you need to improve upon.

4 Flood disaster

How do people cope?

Learn about

Flooding is the worst type of natural disaster. It causes more damage across the world than any other hazard. Understanding the causes and effects of floods can help people to manage the problems that they create. In this unit you will learn:

- what happens to water when it lands on the ground
- what causes floods
- how people respond to floods
- how the effects of flooding in the United Kingdom are different from those in Mozambique.

A

In February 2000, Mozambique, a country in south-east Africa, suffered devastating flooding. Look carefully at photograph **A** on the opposite page. The dry land around the base of the tree is keeping a family safe from the flooded rivers.

Activities

1. Work in pairs to answer the following questions.

   a Who do you think took this photograph?

   b What might the view from the top of the tree look like?

   c How many people are on the dry land in the photograph?

   d How big do you think the piece of dry land is?

   e Name five things, other than people, that are on the dry land.

   f Why do you think these things were important enough for the family to save?

   g Name three things in the tree.

   h Why do you think they have put these things in the tree?

   i What other things, that cannot be seen, will the family need to survive?

   j Where will they go to the toilet?

   k Why might this cause problems?

   l Is the weather warm or cold?

   m What is the evidence for this?

   n What shelter does the family have?

   o Why might this be a problem?

   p Why might these people be waiting, rather than trying to escape?

   q Who might rescue them, and how?

2. Do you think Mozambique is a rich or a poor country?

3. Give three reasons why it is difficult for Mozambique to cope with floods.

In 1998 large areas of the United Kingdom were affected by flooding. Over the Easter holiday, flooding caused damage worth £400 million, five people died and more than 1500 people were **evacuated** from their homes. Then, in October 1998, about 8000 square kilometres of England and Wales were flooded. The River Wye was 5 metres above its winter level and more than 160 kilometres of the River Severn were on red flood warning alert (see page 80 for a definition). Two thousand homes were cut off by flood water for two days.

Activities

4. Using the questions in activity **1** above to help you, write down five geographical questions you could ask someone about photograph **B**.

5. Swap questions with another person. Answer each other's questions.

6. In a pair, compare your questions and decide on the best five. Write down what you think makes a good geographical question.

7. a The United Kingdom is a much richer country than Mozambique. Does this mean that the effects of floods will be worse than in Mozambique?

   b Give reasons for your answer.

Understanding flooding: what happens to water when it reaches the ground?

Water that falls from the sky is called **precipitation**. This rain, snow or hail is part of a never-ending process called the **water cycle.** Figure **A** shows a simple version of this cycle. Water evaporates from the sea, then the vapour rises and **condenses** to form clouds. The water in the clouds then falls back to the ground as precipitation, before flowing back to the sea. To understand how flooding is caused, it is important to understand what happens to water when it reaches the ground. When precipitation lands on the Earth's surface, it will either:

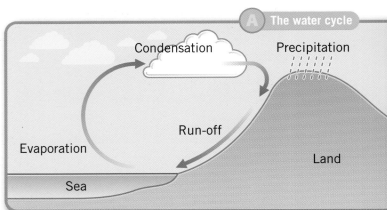

A   The water cycle

Condensation   Precipitation

Run-off

Evaporation

Land

Sea

- **infiltrate** (sink) into the soil and rock. Here it will either flow as groundwater into a river, or be used by plants that then **transpire** the water
- lie on the surface of the ground in a puddle or a lake and eventually **evaporate**
- flow over the surface of the ground as **surface run-off**.

Whether or not the water infiltrates depends on many different factors, such as:

- if the ground is **permeable** or **impermeable**
- if the ground is flat or sloping
- how heavily the rain is falling.

Water which flows over the land as surface run-off tends to reach rivers much more quickly than groundwater.

Getting Technical ▾

Precipitation

Water falling from the air to Earth as rain, hail, sleet or snow.

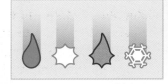

Evaporation

The change of water from a liquid, which is visible, to water vapour, which is an invisible gas.

Transpiration

Water vapour given off by plants into the air.

Condensation

The change of invisible water vapour in the air into liquid droplets which are visible as cloud.

Surface run-off

The flow of water over the ground surface, including rivers and streams.

Groundwater flow

The slow flow of water beneath the surface, through soil and rocks.

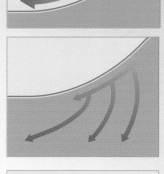

Infiltration

When water sinks into the ground.

Permeable

Ground that allows water to pass through it.

Impermeable

Ground that does not allow water to pass through it.

Activity

Fieldwork enquiry
Asking questions

You are going to investigate one big enquiry question:

> **What happens to water when it reaches the ground?**

① You can do some fieldwork on different surfaces in your school grounds to investigate these geographical questions.

What happens to water when:

a it lands on a flat surface?

b it lands on a sloping surface?

c it lands on a permeable surface such as grass or soil?

d it lands on an impermeable surface such as concrete or tarmac?

e it falls quickly or heavily?

f it falls slowly or gently?

❷ Collecting information

a Go out into your school grounds with a watering-can full of water and carry out research into questions **1a–f** above. Observe the water landing on different types of surface at different rates (heavily and gently). Record exactly what happens each time using words from the Getting Technical box.

b When you get back to the classroom, write the title:

What happens to water when it reaches the ground?

❸ Presenting your results

a Make a large copy of the table below to show your results. Fill in as many boxes as you can. Include drawings to show what happened in each place where you poured the water.

	Permeable surface	Impermeable surface	Heavy downpour	Light downpour
Flat surface				
Sloping surface				

b Find a way to show the results on a map of your school

❹ Describing and explaining your results

Write the side-heading *Conclusions*. For each of the six questions **1a–f** opposite, describe what happened and give as many reasons for this as you can. You *must* use the following words in your answers:

infiltrate   **permeable**
impermeable   **surface run-off**

❺ a Look again at your table and choose the three factors that help water **infiltrate** into the ground.

b Choose the three factors that help water **run-off** the surface.

What causes the River Severn in the United Kingdom to flood?

A River Severn flooding west of Shrewsbury in 1998

The town of Shrewsbury is built on the banks of the River Severn in Shropshire (see page 81). The River Severn is famous for its flooding. One flood in 1795 destroyed most of the bridges on the River Severn. The river floods when there is too much water for the channel to hold. The water then overflows the river banks and floods onto the flood plain in the river valley. River flooding is caused by a combination of physical and human factors.

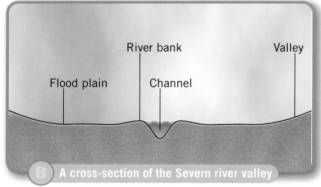

B A cross-section of the Severn river valley

Factors that cause the River Severn to flood

The amount of precipitation

The month of October 1998 was one of the wettest ever recorded. In Wales, where the River Severn has its source, 135 mm of rain fell. This was twice as much as usual. The ground was already very wet when heavy rainstorms fell on 22nd October. The ground could not absorb any more water.

The size of the drainage basin

The area of land drained by a river and its tributaries is called its **drainage basin**. The River Severn's drainage basin is 11 400 km^2, the biggest in England and Wales. It therefore collects more rainfall than smaller drainage basins.

The steepness of the slopes

The River Severn begins its journey to the sea in the mountains of Wales. A lot of the land here is very steep, so water flows quickly into the river.

The type of vegetation (plants)

Most of the River Severn's drainage basin is covered by moorland and grassland. This type of **vegetation** does not use up and transpire as much water as trees. The basin was once covered in woodland, but people have cut down most of the trees to make space for farming.

The number of tributaries

If there are lots of big tributaries in the **drainage basin**, then the water will get to the main river quickly and cause a flood. The River Severn has 12 large tributaries.

Towns and cities

Surfaces in towns and cities have lots of tarmac and concrete. These impermeable surfaces make flooding worse because the water cannot infiltrate into the ground. Instead it runs off into the rivers. Map **A** on page 61 shows that there are lots of big towns, like Shrewsbury and Bridgnorth, along the course of the River Severn.

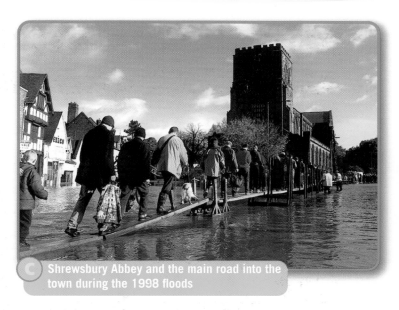
C Shrewsbury Abbey and the main road into the town during the 1998 floods

Activities

1 What is a river flood?

2 a Copy the table below. Write the other physical and human causes of flooding for the River Severn in the correct column.

Physical causes	Human causes
• Heavy rainfall in October 1998	• People built many towns
•	•

b For each of the factors in the table, explain 'so what?', like this:

Heavy rainfall in October 1998.	**So what?**	This meant that the soil was saturated, so rainwater flowed straight into the river.

3 Use map **D** from the *Sunday Telegraph* newspaper to name five of the River Severn's tributaries.

4 Which of these tributaries joins the River Severn before it reaches Shrewsbury?

WHERE THE WASH-OUT IS WORST

MELVERLEY: Severe flooding. Homes abandoned

SHREWSBURY: Worst flooding for more than 30 years with over 200 homes affected

RIVERS WYE /ARROW: About 2000 homes in this area cut off for two days

BRIDGNORTH: Homes flooded

HEREFORD: Roughly 100 properties affected this week

BEWDLEY: Twenty people evacuated. Residents report worst flooding since 1947

ROSS-ON-WYE: More than 30 properties flooded, including old cattle market

Key
● Towns flooded
○ Towns under threat

River Vyrnwy · River Severn · River Terne · River Terne · River Wye · River Arrow · River Lugg · River Wye · Welshpool · Newtown · Telford · Birmingham · Worcester · Tewkesbury · Gloucester · Bristol · ENGLAND · WALES · M6 · M54 · M5 · M4 · M4 · M5

Area of detail · Severn · Wye

0   20 km

D Places affected when the River Severn flooded in 1998, adapted from the *Sunday Telegraph*

5 Name the four towns on the Severn affected by flooding.

6 Study photos **A** and **C**, as well as map **D**. Give five different ways that people in this area were affected by the flooding. You could mention homes, jobs, transport and services.

7 Study photograph **A**. How do you think people living in this area will be affected by floods? Make five suggestions.

What are the effects of the River Severn flooding?

Activities

Getting to know the area on the map

1 The River Severn flows from west to east on the map. Follow the course of the river with your finger from where it appears on the map to where it leaves the map.

   a Is the name of the last village you go past Montford or Emstrey?

   b How many road bridges cross the River Severn on the map?

   c What other type of bridge crosses the River Severn?

   d Which road crosses the River Severn at both grid references 429152 and 522109?

2 The distance along the River Severn between grid references 429152 and 522109 is 40 km.

   a What is the straight line distance in kilometres?

   b How many times longer is the distance along the river than the straight line distance?

   c What does this tell you about the course of the River Severn?

Disaster at Montford Bridge, October 1998

3 **a** *Thursday 22 October: Environment Agency puts Shrewsbury on a red flood warning alert.* What does this mean?

   b *Friday 23 October: At Preston Montford (grid reference 4314) 42 mm of rain has fallen in 24 hours.* Is Preston Montford north, south, east or west of Shrewsbury?

   c *Monday 26 October: The River Severn has flooded many areas of Shrewsbury. Welsh Bridge (grid reference 488127) and English Bridge (grid reference 496124) are closed. The Toll bridge between these bridges is still open.* What is the six-figure grid reference for the Toll bridge?

   d *10.00 a.m. Wednesday 28 October: A phone call tells Shropshire fire and rescue service that fallen trees have jammed under the bridge at Montford Bridge. The rising water behind the bridge could destroy it, sending a wave of flood water down the valley.* What problems could this disaster cause in grid square 4315?

   e *The fire service's heavy lifting gear can only be moved along A and B roads.* What colours are A and B roads on the OS map?

   f *The fire station is at grid reference 496135. The rescue team must reach Montford Bridge quickly to save the bridge.* Work out the best route for the fire engine to take.

Environment Agency – Levels of flood warning

Yellow Warning: flooding to roads and low-lying land from wind-blown spray.

Amber Warning: flooding to isolated properties, roads and large areas of farmland near rivers.

Red Warning: serious flooding affecting many properties, roads and areas of farmland near rivers.

Don't forget that some bridges are closed.

KEY

Railway	Road bridge
A 572 A road	Bridge
B 5204 B road	Railway bridge
Dual carriageway	Church
Caravan site	Contour
Camp site	Public House
PH Public House	50

0 1km
0 2cm

How do people respond to floods in the United Kingdom?

Activities

1 Use a long ruler to measure a depth of 60 cm. Imagine that your home gets flooded with water this deep.

  a What would get soaking wet in your house, and how would it be damaged? Make a list of all the problems that this water would cause, both inside and outside your home.

  b If the flooding lasts for a week, how would this affect you and your family? Think about your everyday lives.

  c If you were warned that there was going to be a flood, what could you do to reduce the damage? Make a list.

  d Use photo **A,** and your own ideas, to explain how the emergency services can help people when there is a flood.

2 a Read the story of Fiona and Mark Dodd and the 1998 floods.

  b Make a large copy of the table below. Write in what the Dodds did before, during and after the flood and what they felt.

	Before the flood started (at midnight on Friday night)	During the flood	On Monday and after the flood
What Fiona and Mark Dodds *did*			
What Fiona and Mark Dodds *felt*			

  c Make a list of all the people and organisations that are mentioned in the story. Next to each one say whether they helped the Dodds and what they did:

People/organisation	Did they help?	What did they do?
Weather forecasters and Environment Agency	Yes	Said that rain was forecast and gave a flood warning
Police officer	Yes	

A Firefighters organising a rescue in flooded Leamington Spa, 1998

Fiona and Mark Dodd and the 1998 floods

In the weeks before Easter 1998 it rained very heavily across England and Wales. On *Thursday 9 April*, one month's rain had fallen in 24 hours, and heavy rain was forecast for most of Friday and Saturday in the Midlands.

Fiona and Mark Dodd live with their two young children in Far Cotton near Northampton, close to the River Nene. They did not like the weather forecast, but they were not worried about a flood, so they did not do anything. Just after *midnight*, early on *Friday 10 April*, a policeman called to say that the Environment Agency had put out a flood warning. Half an hour later polluted water swept through the houses in their village. Within minutes the water was 30 cm deep so Mark took the children upstairs. Fiona tried to keep the rising water out with a bucket and pans ... but it was hopeless. They rang Mark's brother, who lives 3 miles away, but he couldn't drive beyond the end of his flooded street.

At *2.00 a.m.* the flood water cut off the power supply. The Dodds tried to move their most valuable possessions upstairs in the dark but in the panic their wedding photographs and earliest pictures of their children were lost. 'How can I tell my daughter as she grows up that I have no photographs of her as a baby?' Fiona cried to a BBC news reporter the following day. 'Our furniture, carpets, washing-machine, television ... everything downstairs is ruined. Our sense of security has been shattered in a terrifying seven hours of cold, wet, pitch-blackness.' Mrs Scott, an elderly neighbour, was filmed as she was carried out of her house by paramedics. She was suffering from hypothermia.

Northamptonshire County Council arranged for flood victims to move into the primary school hall in the next village for the *Easter weekend*. Social Services provided the Dodds and other families with blankets and hot meals.

On *Monday* the Anglian Water Authority pumped the water from the Dodds' street. It smelled awful because of the sewage in it. On *Tuesday* the electrician isolated the sockets downstairs so that the electricity upstairs could

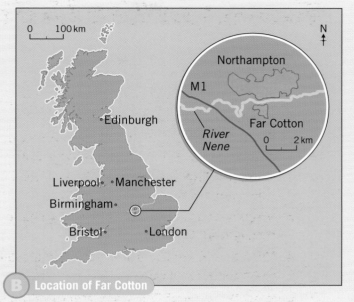

B Location of Far Cotton

be turned on. The assessor from the insurance company came on the *Thursday* and agreed that they needed new carpets.

Over the *next three weeks* Fiona and Mark had to strip the floors down to bare concrete and take the plaster off the walls. Fiona found the constant noise of four dehumidifiers and air-movers very stressful. Their daily struggles with their insurance company and bank put them both under a huge strain.

Mark was critical about the lack of help from the local council: 'Since the flood, we have had no information on health and hygiene precautions or possible pollution effects, except for one leaflet telling us to wash our hands and wear rubber gloves!' He was also angry to discover that the Environment Agency, in charge of flood defences and warnings, had provided sandbags and boats to other flooded areas.

Three months after the flood Fiona and Mark were still shocked and angry: shocked that their lives could have been devastated by flood water sweeping away their possessions; angry that this could have happened without warning. All they could ask was: 'Why did this happen to us?' and 'Could it happen again?'

• *Based on information from the Environment Agency's Easter 1998 Flood report*

What caused the flooding in Mozambique?

A Mozambique fact file

Area: 801 590 square km (UK 244 100 square km)

Capital: Maputo

Population: 18 million (UK 56 million)

Language: Portuguese, but most people speak local languages, e.g. Swahili

Life expectancy: 47 years

Landscape: Mainly lowland with many large rivers

B

In February 2000, a total of 1163 mm of rain fell, with the area around Maputo getting 455 mm in just three days. This led to the worst flooding in southern Mozambique for 40 years. More than 100 000 hectares of farmland were flooded. By February 20th more than 300 000 people had lost their homes. To make matters worse, **cyclone** Eline hit the coast on February 21st, bringing more rain and strong winds. It destroyed roads, ripped roofs off houses and cut electricity and telephone lines.

C

There was also heavy rain inland. In Zimbabwe, eight metre high waves rushed down the Limpopo and Incomati Rivers and into Mozambique. As there was no warning system between the two countries, the people of Mozambique did nothing to prepare themselves.

In Zambia, Lake Kariba started to overflow, so the giant Kariba Dam was opened to stop the floods. All this extra water flowed down into Mozambique. There was not much vegetation to soak up rain water in Mozambique. Over the years, many plants and trees have been cleared for farmland and settlements.

Activities

1. Create a fact file for Mozambique using an atlas. Use the information in **A** as a starting point. Find information such as *total rainfall, monthly temperatures* and *population density*.

2. **a** Draw a table, like the one below.

Physical causes	Human causes

b Study the factors below. Which of these factors are physical, and which are human? Write each of the causes in the correct column of your table.

heavy rain   no warning   Mozambique is quite flat   there are many large rivers cyclone Eline   not much vegetation the Kariba Dam was opened

The effects of the floods in Mozambique

Joao Nhassengo works in the Johannesburg gold mines in South Africa. He heard about the Mozambique floods on the radio, and rushed home to his village, not knowing whether his family was dead or alive. He found his village underwater and his family gone.

When the water had dropped to waist deep he made his way back to his home, but there was still no word of his family. Then two days ago his wife, Beatriz, returned. 'When I saw her coming across the field on her own, I thought the children must be dead or very sick.' To his joy, he learned that the children had survived and were in a camp.

Now they are all together again. The children have stomach pains caused by drinking the polluted floodwater.

Many of their neighbours have caught cholera from it. Their home is wrecked. The force of the water smashed all the windows and ripped the doors from their hinges. It tore away part of the roof.

But most important are the crops. Beatriz, who is 21, worked a patch of ground nearly five metres wide by 12 metres long. This land fed her family, and, if there was a good harvest, supplied a little extra cash. 'The hoes are still in the house. That is a start, but the maize is ruined.'

'It is something to survive. My children are alive. My house I can rebuild. My crops will grow again. There are many struggles in life. This is just one.'

Adapted from *The Guardian*, Friday 10 March, 2000

The TV cameras have gone but the misery goes on in Mozambique. The water wrecked or damaged the homes of about 250 000 people. Most factories were largely untouched by the floods. However, there was considerable damage to the roads and railways used for trade.

The government estimates that it will need £175 million to rebuild the 620 miles of roads and long stretches of railway track that were swept away. Then there are the electricity and telephone lines and more than 600 schools in need of repair.

Adapted from *The Guardian*, Tuesday 28 March, 2000

TREE PEOPLE FACE WILDLIFE PERIL

Celeste Limbombo said her clothes and head were covered in bugs for days. 'Sometimes I couldn't open my eyes because the insects crawled into them. There was no food and drinking the water made me sick. If you are in a tree you have to do all your private things in front of everybody. If you are young it is easy; you can climb down to the water. If you are old it is very hard to move.'

The Guardian, Saturday 4 March, 2000

A People abandon their homes taking only what they can carry

B Hundreds of people are cut off from the city of Xai-Xai

Activities

1 a If Joao heard about the flood on February 20th, how long was it before he found his family?

b Give three words to describe how he might have felt during this time.

2 What happened to the buildings? Why?

3 Even if people were safe in trees, they still faced problems. Make a list of four different problems.

Forty-one helicopters and 15 planes flying from Maputo and Beira are transporting food and medical supplies. So far 14 000 people have been airlifted to safety by six South African helicopters. But there are too few to pluck all the survivors from the flood and many have lived in trees for days.

One helicopter pilot wept as he described his desperation at being able to save just a few dozen people at a time. 'People are just disappearing. We can't get to them all in time. We see people waving from the roofs of houses and when we fly back they're gone' he said.

One woman threw her baby at a full helicopter as it lifted off. A crew member caught the child but the mother's fate is unknown.

Daily Telegraph, **Tuesday 29 March, 2000**

C Rescue arrives just in time for these flood victims, but they are the lucky ones

D A flooded village near to the Limpopo River

- Britain has donated £5.8 million and cancelled Mozambique's debts.
- British aid included 100 boats and life rafts, 30 emergency rescue workers, a military team, four RAF helicopters and money to hire further helicopters.
- The charities Action Aid, Save the Children, Oxfam, Cafod, Christian Aid, Red Cross, Concern, Help the Aged, Merlin, Tear Fund and World Vision have all helped.
- Italy provided £3.3 million in aid and Japan gave £62,500 in tents and equipment.
- The French relief agency Médecins du Monde sent a five-person team and 10 tonnes of medical equipment.

Activities

1 The Mozambique floods had serious effects. Write out the list of problems and match each one with the correct effect. The first one has been done for you.

Problem	Effect
Homes damaged	so illness and disease is common
Homes destroyed	so people need money for repairs
Possessions lost	so they need to be rescued
Families split up	so families suffer grief and sadness
People stranded in trees and on rooftops	so people are searching for their friends and family
Many people died	so there will be hunger and starvation
Polluted water	so people are homeless
Crops destroyed	so it will cost Mozambique millions to repair
Infrastructure (roads, telephone and electricity lines) destroyed	so people will have to buy or make new things

2 Some of these effects are **short term**, and must be tackled straight away, within a few days. Some will take months or years to solve, so they are **long term**. Colour or highlight the short-term effects in your list.

3 Find three types of aid, sent to Mozambique, that helped the short-term problems. Explain how each one helped the situation.

4 Explain one way that aid can help Mozambique in the long term.

Review and reflect

Flood disaster – how do people cope?

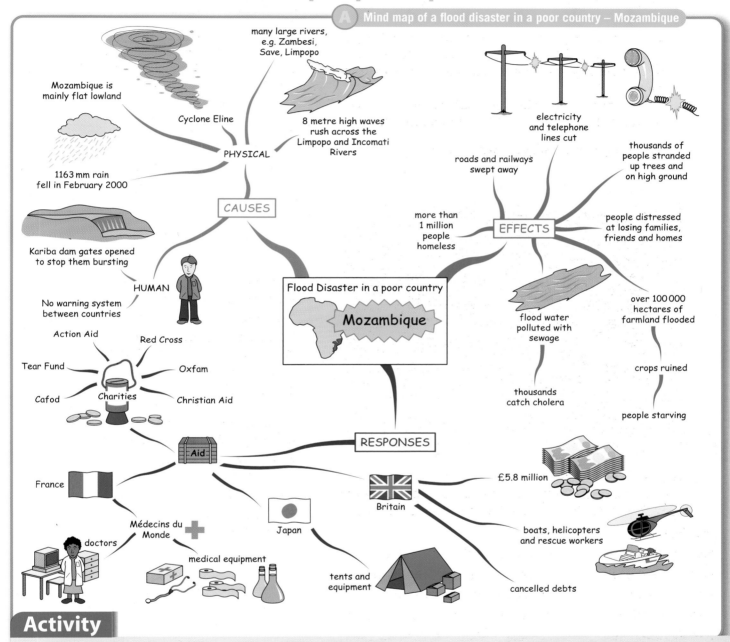

A Mind map of a flood disaster in a poor country – Mozambique

Mozambique is mainly flat lowland

1163 mm rain fell in February 2000

Cyclone Eline

many large rivers, e.g. Zambesi, Save, Limpopo

8 metre high waves rush across the Limpopo and Incomati Rivers

PHYSICAL

CAUSES

Kariba dam gates opened to stop them bursting

No warning system between countries

HUMAN

Action Aid

Tear Fund

Red Cross

Cafod

Charities

Oxfam

Christian Aid

Aid

RESPONSES

France

Médecins du Monde

Japan

doctors

medical equipment

tents and equipment

Britain

£5.8 million

boats, helicopters and rescue workers

cancelled debts

Flood Disaster in a poor country

Mozambique

electricity and telephone lines cut

roads and railways swept away

thousands of people stranded up trees and on high ground

more than 1 million people homeless

EFFECTS

people distressed at losing families, friends and homes

flood water polluted with sewage

over 100 000 hectares of farmland flooded

crops ruined

thousands catch cholera

people starving

Activity

1. Look carefully at the mind map above. It shows information about the flood disaster in Mozambique, a poor country. Use the information from pages 78–83 to design and draw your own mind map for the flooding in the UK, a rich country.

2. At the start of the unit, you were asked whether flooding was worse in the UK or in Mozambique. What did you think? What do you think now?

3. a Do you think that people in different places respond to floods in the same way?

   b Compare the Dodd family (page 83) with the Nhassengo family (page 85). Did they do the same things when their homes flooded?

   c Do emergency services respond in the same way in the UK and Mozambique?

   d Try to explain any differences that you find.

5 Exploring England

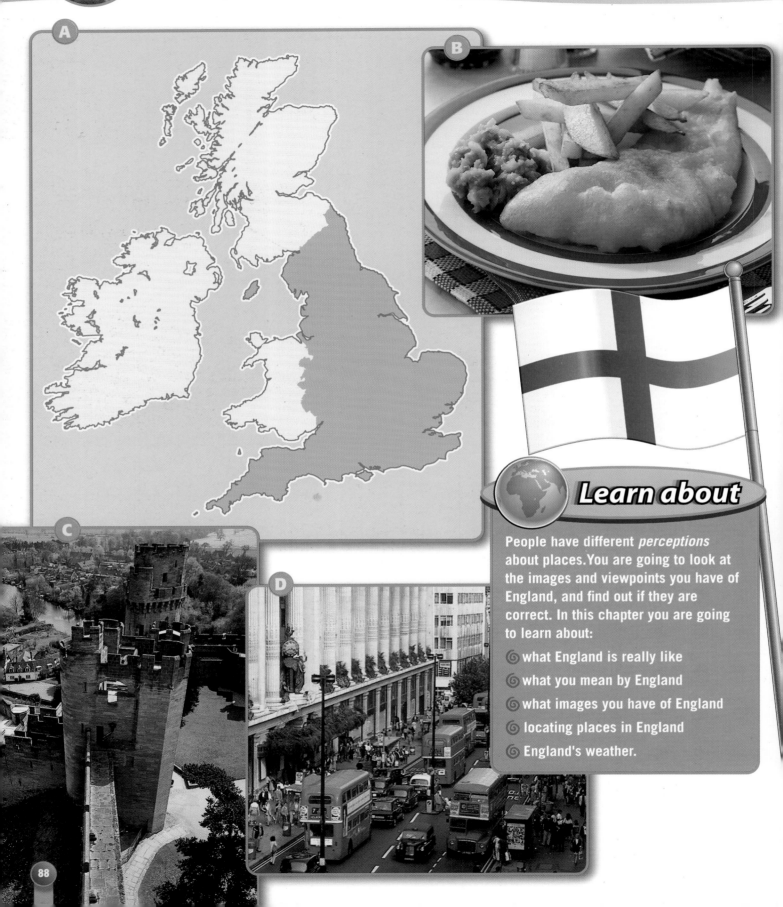

Learn about

People have different *perceptions* about places. You are going to look at the images and viewpoints you have of England, and find out if they are correct. In this chapter you are going to learn about:

⊚ what England is really like

⊚ what you mean by England

⊚ what images you have of England

⊚ locating places in England

⊚ England's weather.

What is England really like?

Jasbir, aged 11

A

" It's not fair that so many people in London are wealthy. "

Kerrie, aged 14

B

" England is a great place, because it's full of old buildings, narrow streets, cathedrals and many attractions. "

C

Heidi, aged 12

" English food is boring – all those fish and chips! "

Asma, aged 13

D

" England is a leading world power. "

Carl, aged 15

E

" Stratford-upon-Avon is the birthplace of William Shakespeare. "

Amy, aged 14

F

" England is a multi-cultural society. "

Joe, aged 17

G

" England has a famous monarchy. "

...tt, aged 11

H

...he River Severn is England's ...gest natural waterway. "

Su-yin, aged 16

I

" English weather is OK – when the rain stops! "

Activities

1 Study quotes **A** to **I** about England and decide which are facts and which are opinions. Organise them into a copy of the table below.

Facts	Opinions

2 Compare your list with a partner. Are they the same? Explain the difference between a fact and an opinion.

3 Choose one fact and one opinion from your list.

  a How did you decide that something was a fact?

  b How did you decide that something was an opinion?

4 Investigate people's viewpoints in your class or family by asking them to 'say three things about England'.

  a How do they compare with the views of people shown here?

  b Why do you think people have different **perceptions** of England?

What do you mean by England?

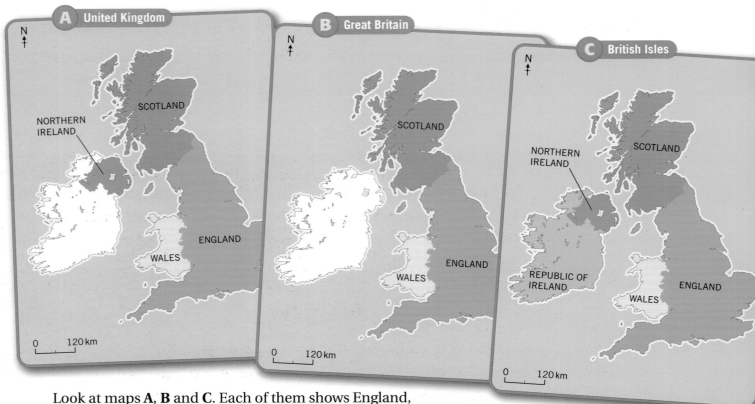

A United Kingdom

N↑

NORTHERN IRELAND

SCOTLAND

ENGLAND

WALES

0   120 km

B Great Britain

N↑

SCOTLAND

ENGLAND

WALES

0   120 km

C British Isles

N↑

NORTHERN IRELAND

SCOTLAND

REPUBLIC OF IRELAND

ENGLAND

WALES

0   120 km

Look at maps **A**, **B** and **C**. Each of them shows England, but they are all slightly different. People often talk about England when they really mean the United Kingdom, Great Britain or the British Isles. So that you do not get these names confused, you are going to look at what each one means.

Activities

1. Draw a large copy of the Venn diagram opposite. Now use maps **A**, **B** and **C** to add the five countries in the correct part of the diagram.

2. In a group, discuss why you think England is part of all three maps **A**, **B** and **C**.

3. Use your Venn diagram and the ideas from your discussion to write a paragraph about England.

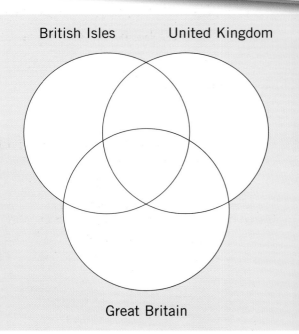

British Isles   United Kingdom

Great Britain

	England	Scotland	Wales	Northern Ireland	Republic of Ireland
Population (millions)	48.5	5	3	1.5	3.5
Area (km²)	130 000	77 000	21 000	13 500	69 000

D Population and area statistics for parts of the British Isles

Activities

1 a Make a copy of the table below.

	England	Scotland	Wales	Northern Ireland	Republic of Ireland
County					
City					
Hills or mountains					
River or lake					

b Look at the following list of 24 places. Decide what they are and put them in the correct box in the table. You might have to use an atlas for some of them.

Thames	Glasgow	London	Loch Ness	Newcastle upon Tyne
Cardiff	Lake District	Cornwall	Grampians	Manchester
Pennines	Belfast	Liverpool	Antrim	Lothian
Edinburgh	Snowdonia	Trent	Clare	Birmingham
Severn	Lough Neagh	Powys	Dublin	

c Think of some important places that have been missed off the list.
Add ten more of your own to the table.

2 Using an outline map of the British Isles, show some of this information. Label:

a England, Scotland, Wales, Northern Ireland and the Republic of Ireland   **b** five rivers
c the place where you live   **d** five upland areas (hills or mountains)   **e**   five cities.
Think carefully how to show each place, using symbols and different colours.

3 Copy out the table below. Complete it by regrouping the information from table **D** opposite.

	England	Great Britain	United Kingdom	British Isles
Population (millions)				
Area (km²)				

4 Think of a way of showing this population and area information on some graphs. Here is one idea to get you started:

5 Write five bulleted statements to summarise what the table and graphs tell you about the population and area in England, Great Britain, the United Kingdom and the British Isles.

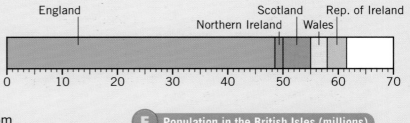

E Population in the British Isles (millions)

6 **Extension**
England, the United Kingdom, Great Britain and the British Isles make up parts of Europe and the whole world. Using symbols or a map, show how:
a England is part of Europe   **b** England is part of the world.

Try to think creatively and be imaginative in how you represent the connections.

What images do you have of England?

Activities

1 Look at images **A** to **I**. Decide which of these categories each image belongs to:

- 🌀 definitely in England
- 🌀 unlikely to be in England
- 🌀 probably in England
- 🌀 definitely not in England.

2 Share your ideas with the rest of your group. Be prepared to *justify* your ideas.

3 Look at the images that you decided were 'definitely' or 'probably' in England. For each one, write two things that it tells you about England.

4 Now choose one image that you think is the most accurate reflection of what England is like. Answer these questions.

- **a** How can you tell that it is in England?
- **b** Where might it be in England?
- **c** Who would go to this place?
- **d** Will this place always be like this?
- **e** What impressions does this image give you?

Where are you in England?

To identify places, you need to think about their characteristics and features. Every place is unique, from the largest city to the smallest village. The place where you live has its own identity.

Activities

1 Where am I?

This place:

- was known as 'the city of a thousand trades'
- is famous for its balti restaurants
- has more canals than Venice
- is home to the International Convention Centre
- has a Premier League football team based at Villa Park
- is where Cadbury's chocolate originated
- has a well known road network nicknamed 'Spaghetti Junction'
- is England's second city
- is home to people who are often called 'Brummies'.

2 Each member of a group in turn thinks of a place. The rest of the group must try to find out the identity of the place by asking questions. They must guess the place within ten questions. The help box gives you suggestions of how to ask questions.

ICT Research activity

3 Investigate the images Birmingham presents of itself on the Internet: www.birmingham.gov.uk.

help!

There are many different ways of finding out information. To find out more about a place, you could start your questions with the words:

- ✪ What ...?
- ✪ Where ...?
- ✪ When ...?
- ✪ Why ...?
- ✪ Who ...?

See also page 10.

What is the weather like?

Weather in the British Isles is changeable – it is always changing. It can be rainy, sunny, cold or warm, sometimes all on the same day. The British **climate** is called **temperate** because of its mild and moist weather.

Activities

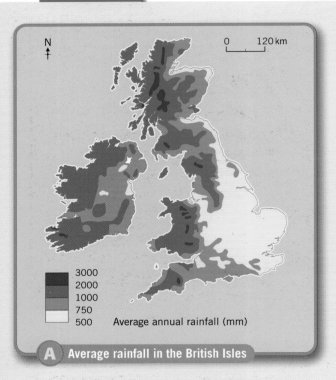

3000
2000
1000
750
500   Average annual rainfall (mm)

A Average rainfall in the British Isles

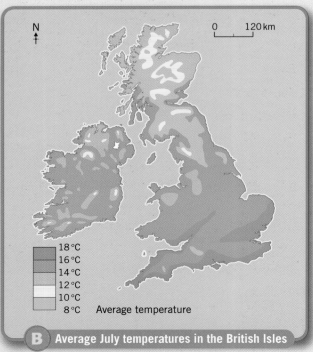

18 °C
16 °C
14 °C
12 °C
10 °C
8 °C   Average temperature

B Average July temperatures in the British Isles

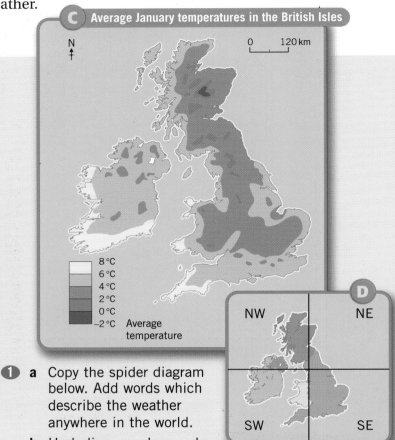

C Average January temperatures in the British Isles

8 °C
6 °C
4 °C
2 °C
0 °C
–2 °C   Average
temperature

D

| NW | NE |
| SW | SE |

1 a Copy the spider diagram below. Add words which describe the weather anywhere in the world.

b Underline or colour-code words which are true of weather in the British Isles. Discuss your choice with a partner – how did you make the selection?

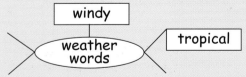

windy

weather words

tropical

2 a In pairs, divide a blank map of the British Isles into four areas, like the one in **D**.

b For one area (NW, NE, SW or SE) use maps **A**, **B** and **C** to describe the weather characteristics of the region. You can use words or symbols to show the weather characteristics on your own map. Here are some words and phrases you could use.

**wettest   driest   warmest region in summer
mild winters**

c Share your information with others to complete your map of the British Isles. Label or draw the information onto your map.

Location	Average annual rainfall (mm)	Height of land above sea level (m)
Scafell Pike	2500	978
The Fens (East Anglia)	600	0
South Downs	750	255
Chiltern Hills	650	240
Pennines	1200	693
Cheviot Hills	1000	816
Dartmoor	1500	621

E Rainfall and height above sea level for some English locations

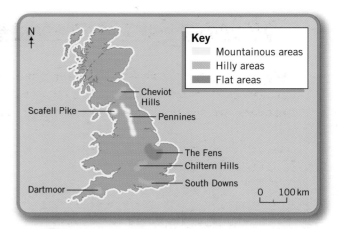

Key
- Mountainous areas
- Hilly areas
- Flat areas

Cheviot Hills
Scafell Pike
Pennines
The Fens
Chiltern Hills
South Downs
Dartmoor

0   100 km

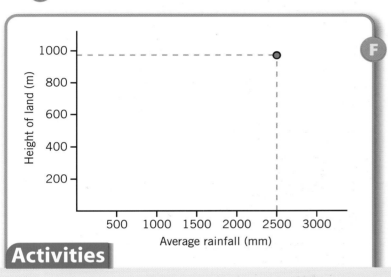

F

How to …

… draw a scattergraph

1 Label the vertical (*y*) axis with the height of the land (m).

2 Label the horizontal (*x*) axis with the average rainfall (mm).

3 For Scafell Pike:
- go up the *y* axis to 978 m.
- go along the *x* axis to 2500 mm.
- plot a point where the two lines meet.

Activities

3 Use maps **B** and **C** to compare the temperatures in winter and summer.
You can use these ideas to get you started.

In general, summer temperatures are…
It is especially warm in the _____ region,
where average temperatures reach _____°C

In winter…

4 Study the figures in table **E**. Plot the values for each place onto a scattergraph of rainfall and height like the one if **F**. The How to … box shows you what to do. ①②③

5 **a** Look carefully at your graph. Can you see a relationship between rainfall and the height of the land?

b Write a summary of the relationship between rainfall and height of the land. You could start like this:

The higher the land…

6 **a** Make a large copy of the table below. Use an atlas, and the information on these pages, to fill in the boxes in the table.

Relief:	Mountainous	Hilly	Flat
Rainfall			
Population			
Other features, e.g roads			

b What relationships can you see between different factors in the table? Look at these, and then find some others.

- relief and rainfall
- population and relief

c Can you give any reasons for the relationships that you found in question b?

Getting Technical ▼

You will find more information about weather in England at www.meto.gov.uk

Why does Britain's weather change?

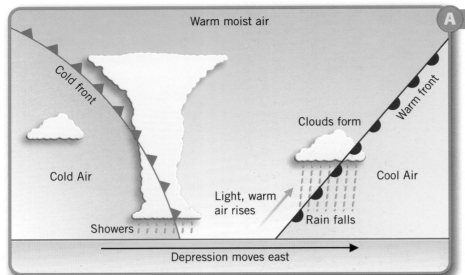

A A cross-section through a depression

Warm moist air

Cold front

Clouds form

Warm front

Cold Air

Cool Air

Light, warm air rises

Rain falls

Showers

Depression moves east

Britain's weather is influenced by two types of **weather systems**:

- **anticyclones** (high pressure) bring settled weather – hot in summer, cold in winter

- **depressions** (low pressure) bring changeable weather – often rain, cloud and wind.

Depressions form over the Atlantic Ocean and move from west to east towards the British Isles. The low pressure draws in warm moist air from the south, and cold air from the north. The warm and cold air masses meet along a long boundary called a **front**.

Depressions can take three days to blow across the British Isles, and they can bring several weather fronts with them. Figure **A** shows what happens at weather fronts.

- Warm air is lighter, so it is forced up over the cold air mass.

- As the warm air rises, it cools down. Moisture condenses to form clouds, which often bring rain.

- Air is sucked into the low pressure system, causing winds which can sometimes be very strong.

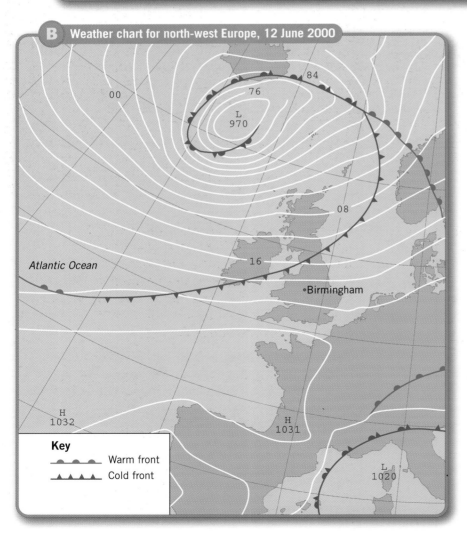

B Weather chart for north-west Europe, 12 June 2000

L 970

84

76

00

08

16

Atlantic Ocean

•Birmingham

H 1032

H 1031

L 1020

Key

⌣⌣⌣ Warm front

▲▲▲ Cold front

Activities

1 Look at Map **B**. It is a **synoptic chart** for north-west Europe on 12th June 2000. There is a depression with very low pressure (970 mb).

   a Where was the depression located on the 12th June?

   b What is the highest pressure on this synoptic chart?

   c Where was this anticyclone located on the 12th June?

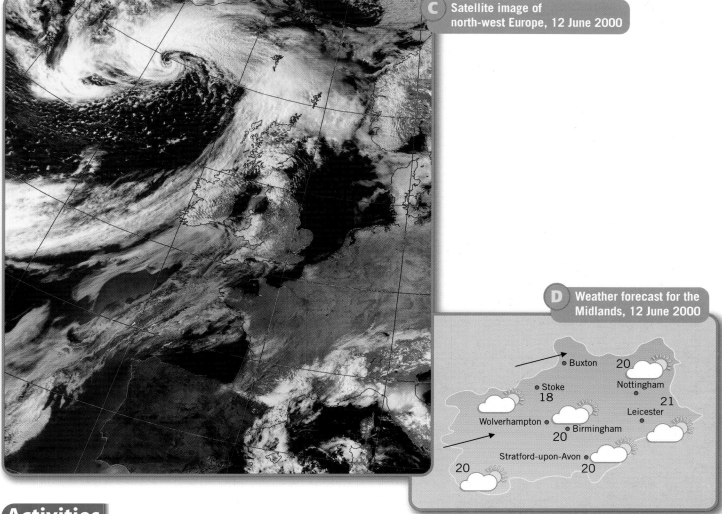

C Satellite image of north-west Europe, 12 June 2000

D Weather forecast for the Midlands, 12 June 2000

- Buxton 20
- Stoke 18
- Nottingham
- 21
- Leicester
- Wolverhampton
- Birmingham 20
- Stratford-upon-Avon 20
- 20
- 20

Activities

2 Use the information on figure **A** and map **B** to describe the weather during a depression. Use these headings to help:

- ⑤ pressure
- ⑤ wind
- ⑤ rainfall.

3 **a** Study map **B**. Make a tracing to show:

- ⑤ the fronts
- ⑤ the low pressure
- ⑤ the high pressure.

b Add some weather labels to your tracing:

- ⑤ warm and cold air
- ⑤ high and low pressure
- ⑤ rain
- ⑤ clear sky
- ⑤ windy.

c Now try to explain some of this weather. Label the reasons onto your tracing.

4 In groups of five or six, plan a mime of the processes involved in the formation and development of a depression. Use the key words from the text and your answers to activities **2–4** to help you. Show your mime to the rest of the class, then use key words to explain what is happening.

5 **Extension**
Study weather map **D** for the West Midlands.
a Describe the weather on Monday 12 June.
b Use satellite image **C** and synoptic chart **B** to forecast what you think will happen to the weather on Tuesday 13 June.
c Draw a simple weather map for the weather forecast on Tuesday, 13th June.

Planning a tour of England

MEMORANDUM

FROM: *Area Manager*

TO: *Tour operator*

A party of 50 visitors from the United States will be arriving at Heathrow Airport, London on Monday at 7.00 am. They are in England for five days, and need to return to London on Friday night.

They want a five-day coach tour that will take them to at least seven typically English attractions. Please design their trip and get back to me as soon as possible.

Please note that the group can only travel 300 km (180 miles) per day, so timings are very important.

You will also need to think about the weather people might encounter in different parts of England in June. Think carefully about departure times and the routes used – make these clear on your plan.

Good luck!

A

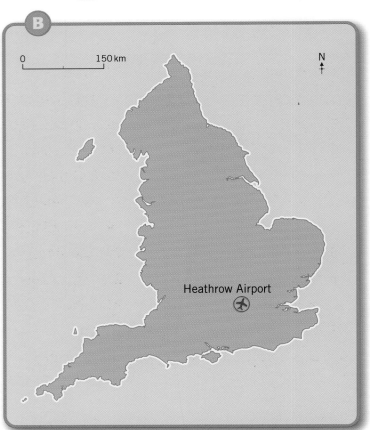

B

Activities

1 Read the memo from Sunshine Tours **(A)**.
   a In pairs, plan a five-day coach tour that will meet all the requirements. Use the Help! box to organise your work.

   b On a map of England, show the five days travel along with:

   ⊚ places to stay on each night

   ⊚ attractions to visit

   ⊚ distances travelled

   ⊚ departure times each day.

   Use a different colour for each day.

2 Research activity

Explore England on the Internet at www.travelengland.org.uk. Choose one region or place you think visitors from the USA might visit on their tour. **ICT**

3 Extension

Use a desktop publishing package to publish an advertising poster or leaflet about your tour. **ICT**

4 Create a word bank of the words you have learned in this unit about England. 📖

help!

When you do an activity, there is a **process of thinking** that helps you to organise your work. Follow these steps in your work:

✪ **plan** Think about what you could include in your tour.

✪ **draft** Decide on the seven (or more) places and organise them into five days. Plan the route. Do a rough copy of your ideas.

✪ **check** Check that your tour meets all the requirements in the memo. Do you need to add anything or cut out something? Do your neat copy.

✪ **evaluate** Has your tour worked? Check with your teacher and with others. What was good about it? Could it have been improved?

Review and reflect

Odd one out

1	Perceptions	13	Wales	25	Relief
2	England	14	Northern Ireland	26	Places
3	Images	15	Republic of Ireland	27	Facts
4	The Lake District	16	The Fens	28	Opinions
5	United Kingdom	17	Weather	29	Plan
6	Great Britain	18	Temperate	30	Check
7	British Isles	19	Anticyclone	31	Evaluate
8	The Pennines	20	Locations	32	Draft
9	Dartmoor	21	Depression	33	Destinations
10	Mountainous	22	Hilly	34	Wind
11	Climate	23	Flat	35	Temperature
12	Scotland	24	Pressure	36	Rainfall

Activities

❶ In pairs, look at each set of numbers below. For each set:
   a Find the four words in the list above that match the numbers.

   b Try to decide which word is the odd one out.

   c Explain why it is the odd one out and what the other three have in common.

Set A	2	5	12	13
Set B	4	8	9	16
Set C	17	21	10	35
Set D	20	24	26	33
Set E	1	3	27	28

❷ Next, design some other sets of numbers to try out on your partner.

❸ Organise all the words on the list into groups. You may have from three to six groups, each with a descriptive heading or title.

❹ Reflect

Look back at the images of England that have been used in this unit, or in the whole book.
Discuss with a partner:
   ⑥ which places have been included   ⑥ which people have been included

   ⑥ which have been left out   ⑥ which have been left out.

Write a short letter to the authors presenting your findings and your point of view.

World sport

Learn about

Sport is enjoyed by people all over the world. In this unit you will learn:

- ⦿ how people take part in or watch sport
- ⦿ why the football industry is changing, and the effects this may have
- ⦿ where football grounds are located, and the reasons for this
- ⦿ how football grounds have an impact on people and environments
- ⦿ how to investigate patterns or changes in sport.

A Sport is important to large international companies ...

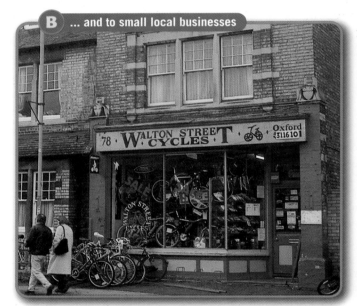

B ... and to small local businesses

C People like to watch sport ...

D ... and to take part themselves

How important is sport?

Sport is an athletic activity, a game or a pastime. Some sports, such as fishing, are done by individual people. Other sports, such as football or netball, are team events. People take part in sport to have fun, to keep fit, to make friends, to compete against others, or to relax.

Sport is becoming more important every year because, as countries develop, many people have more free time and more money to spend. One way to enjoy free time and spend money is to play or watch a sport.

Sport is big business worldwide and involves companies of all sizes. **Multinational** corporations such as Nike, BSkyB and Coca-Cola invest hundreds of millions of pounds in sport every year (see **A**), while small local shops sell fishing tackle and tyre-repair kits (**B**).

Sport brings pleasure to people who watch it (see table **E**). Adults and children also enjoy actively taking part in sport, although there are some differences in the sports they prefer (table **F**). However, people's lives in the UK are changing. Between 1990 and 2000, fewer people went to watch big sporting events, and fewer actively took part in sport.

Sport	Percentage of adults
Football	12.2
Cricket	3.7
Horse racing	3.4
Rugby Union	3.4
Motor racing	3.1

E The top five sports that adults paid to watch (1998)

Aged 11–14		Adults	
Cycling	48	Walking	22
Swimming	41	Aerobics, keep fit, gym	20
Football	33	Swimming	18
Tennis	25	Cycling	9
Walking	18	Golf	8

Figures are percentages that take part in the sport. Some people do more than one sport.

F Taking part: the top five sports in the UK (1998)

Activities

1. Study the photos on the opposite page and discuss these questions with a partner.

   a How many photos are about people actively taking part in sport?

   b Which photos are about team sports?

   c Why are there so many names on the racing car?

   d Give five ways that money and sport are linked in these photos.

2. **a** Choose the type of graph that would best show the data in table **E**.

   b Draw the graph and describe what it shows.

   c Choose a different style of graph that would best show the data in table **F**.

   d Draw the graph and describe what it shows.

3. Do a survey to investigate the sporting activities of the people in your class. Look back at the questionnaire on page 12. These questions may also help you.

   ⑥ Do people do different sporting activities in school, compared with 'out of school'?

   ⑥ Are children's sporting activities different from adults'?

   ⑥ Are sporting activities different for girls and boys?

   ⑥ Do activities vary according to where people live?

help!

Remember the four steps in an enquiry (see pages 10–17):

- ✪ first ask questions
- ✪ then collect information
- ✪ show your results
- ✪ finally make your conclusions.

Football – the world's favourite sport

In terms of business, football is certainly the biggest sport in the world. The 'world game' is the most popular sport on Earth. The World Cup finals have the largest audience of any televised event in the world, and even countries such as the USA and China, not traditional footballing nations, are big fans. It is estimated that football generates £123 billion of economic activity each year.

Football was first played in Britain in the 1870s, and England's Premiership League is among the most famous in the world. The Premiership League includes teams from England and possibly Wales. Scotland has its own league, as do Northern Ireland and the Republic of Ireland.

Arsenal (North London)	Leicester City
Aston Villa (Birmingham)	Liverpool
Bradford	Manchester City
Charlton Athletic (South-east London)	Manchester United
Chelsea (West London)	Middlesbrough
Coventry City	Newcastle United
Derby County	Southampton
Everton (Liverpool)	Sunderland
Ipswich Town	Tottenham Hotspur (North London)
Leeds United	West Ham United (East London)

A The teams in the Premiership League for 2000–2001

Manchester United is one of the most successful and famous of all football teams. You can find their website at http://www.manutd.com.

Table **B** shows that their players come from lots of different countries. This is because Manchester United wants the best players, but it also helps to sell the club's products around the world. For example, if Manchester United were to buy a famous Brazilian player, then sales of their goods in South America would go up.

Manchester United won the European Champions Cup in 1999 for the first time since 1968. Their route to the final is shown in **C**.

Player	Country of origin
Mark Bosnich	Australia
Gary Neville	England
Jaap Stam	Holland (Netherlands)
Mikael Silvestre	France
Philip Neville	England
Paul Scholes	England
Dwight Yorke	Trinidad and Tobago
Roy Keane	Republic of Ireland
Denis Irwin	Republic of Ireland
Ryan Giggs	Wales
Nicky Butt	England
Quinton Fortune	South Africa
Teddy Sheringham	England
Andy Cole	England
Ole Gunnar Solskjaer	Norway
David Beckham	England
Jordi Cruyff	Holland (Netherlands)
Ronny Johnsen	Denmark
Raimond Van der Gouw	Holland (Netherlands)
Wes Brown	England
Ronnie Wallwork	England
Jonathan Greening	England
Alex Ferguson (Manager)	Scotland

B The countries of origin of Manchester United squad, 1999–2000

C Manchester United's European Cup campaign, 1998–1999

Preliminary round

Łódż (Poland)

Group round

Brondby (Sweden)
Bayern Munich (Germany)
Barcelona (Spain)

Quarter Final

Inter Milan (Italy)

Semi Final

Juventus (Turin, Italy)

Final

Bayern Munich (Germany): match played in Barcelona

D The Manchester United team, before playing against Real Madrid in the Opel Masters 2000 Tournament in Munich

Activities

1 On an outline map of England and Wales, plot the *distribution* of football teams in the 2000–2001 Premiership League from table **A**. Think of a suitable way of showing each team.

2 Look at your map and describe the distribution of Premiership teams. Use as many of these words as you can.

**the majority   most   all   some   none
big cities   north   south   Midlands**

3 On an outline map of the world, show the origins of the Manchester United players from Table **B**.

  b What do you notice about the distribution on this map? Make two statements.

4 In every round of the European Cup except the Final, teams play one match at home and one away against each opposing team.

  a Look at **C** and a map of Europe, to see where Manchester United played their away matches in 1998–1999.

  b In how many countries did they play?

  c Which was the furthest match from their home in Manchester?

  d Which was the nearest?

  e How do you think that the team and the supporters travelled to the away games?

ICT Research activity

5 Bring your work up to date by doing some research. Use team websites or newspapers to help you. Choose a league team you support or that plays near your home.

  a Find out the countries of origin of the players in your team. Compare them with those for Manchester United in question **4**.

  b Draw a map to show how your team, or your national team, played their way through another international competition. Follow the steps in question **5**.

Getting to a football match

Following a football team and travelling to their away matches can be quite expensive, and it certainly needs some careful planning. You may have to travel from one end of the country to another to follow your favourite team. You need to decide which type of transport suits your needs, and which is the cheapest.

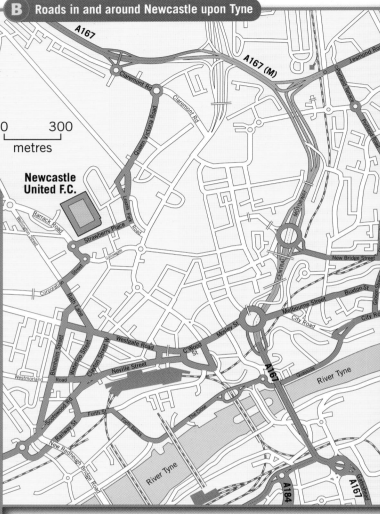

B Roads in and around Newcastle upon Tyne

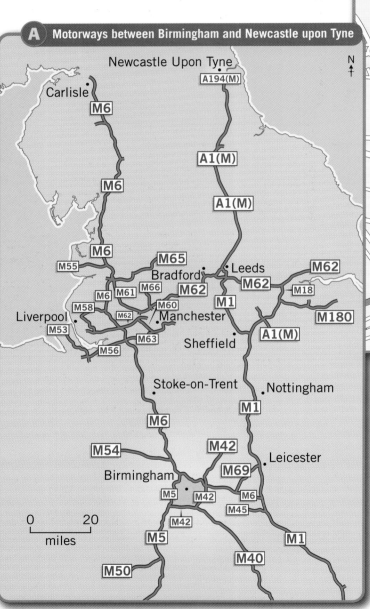

A Motorways between Birmingham and Newcastle upon Tyne

The Third Round of the Cup

Imagine that you live in Birmingham and your team has been drawn to play away against Newcastle United in the FA Cup. You live on the north side of Birmingham close to the M6, and your family decides to drive to Newcastle upon Tyne using the motorway network shown in map **A**.

Activities

1. Describe the route you would take from Birmingham to Newcastle to watch the football match. Look carefully at **B**, which shows roads in and around Newcastle. To get into Newcastle you follow the A184 from the A194 (M).

The Fourth Round of the Cup

After beating Newcastle United your team now has to play away against Chelsea. This time your family decides to take the train. You have to travel by train from Birmingham New Street to London (see **C**) and then take a London Underground train to Fulham Broadway, the nearest station to Chelsea's ground at Stamford Bridge (see **D**).

© London Regional Transport

D London Underground map

Key to lines

▬▬▬	Bakerloo
▬▬▬	Central
▬▬▬	peak hours only
▬▬▬	Circle
▬▬▬	District
▬▬▬	restricted service
▬▬▬	East London
▬▬▬	peak hours and Sunday mornings
▬▬▬	Hammersmith & City
▬▬▬	peak hours only
▬▬▬	Jubilee
▬▬▬	under construction

Activities

2 a How many stations will you pass through, between Birmingham New Street and London Marylebone?

b Look at map **D** of the underground. Write out your route from Marylebone to Fulham Broadway. Include the different underground lines and the stations that you need to use.

c Give one reason why it is easier to go by train than to go by car to Chelsea's ground.

3 Look at the table below, comparing the two away trips.

	Newcastle United	Chelsea
Distance from home in Birmingham	320 km	200 km
Cost of petrol (at 8p per km)	£25.60 each way	£16.00 each way
Train time	3 hours	1 hour 50 minutes (fast) 2 hours 30 minutes (slow)
Train cost (return ticket)	£60	£23.50 (fast) £13.90 (slow)

C Trains from Birmingham to London

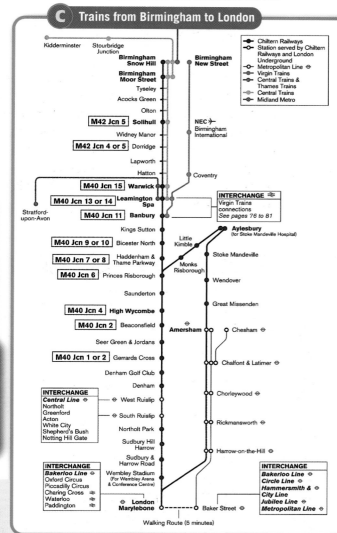

a If a car travels at an average speed of 80 km/hour, how long will it take to travel from Birmingham to:
  ⑥ Newcastle   ⑥ Chelsea?

b Is it quicker to go by train or car to:
  ⑥ Newcastle   ⑥ Chelsea?

c How much will the petrol cost to drive:
  ⑥ to Newcastle and back
  ⑥ to Chelsea and back?

d What other costs do you think are involved in driving a car?

4 There are lots of things that affect how you choose to travel.

In a group, discuss how these factors would affect your decision:

a you have a family of four   **c** safety

b pollution is a concern   **d** convenience

Football – a changing industry

Football attendances

The 1949–50 football season holds the record for attendance at league matches in Britain, with over 40 million people. By the 1985–1986 season this had dropped to 16 million. This 60% fall has been blamed on hooliganism at football matches, and the fact that people were attracted to other types of leisure activities. Attendances have steadily increased since 1986, as football grounds have become safer.

Football crowds are also changing. In the past, most fans came from working class backgrounds. Nowadays Premiership clubs attract more wealthy supporters, as facilities are improved and the cost of tickets has risen. Some people say that only wealthy people can afford to watch the big clubs play.

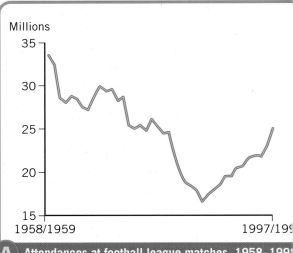

A Attendances at football league matches, 1958–199

Funding

Football teams cost a lot to run, and many clubs make a loss. Players' wages, transfer fees, facilities and equipment all cost a lot of money. Clubs receive income from several sources:

⊚ Sponsorship – clubs earn money through shirt sponsorship. This gives the sponsor much publicity, which is great if the club is doing well. Match programmes can also be sponsored. Money can be made from corporate hospitality, where companies pay to use the club's facilities to entertain customers.

⊚ Advertising – clubs sell advertising space on boards that surround the pitch and in the match programme.

⊚ Ticket sales – the money taken at the gates for league matches is kept by the home team. Small clubs only take a small amount of money. In the FA Cup and Coca-Cola Cup, the ticket money is shared between the teams, so a small club that plays a big club may earn a large sum of money.

⊚ Television fees – about £25 million is available to clubs in the Nationwide League from the TV companies.

- 75 per cent goes to Division One clubs
- 18 per cent goes to Division Two clubs
- 7 per cent goes to Division Three clubs.

BSkyB paid the Premiership League a huge £670 million to televise matches live in the 2000–2001 season.

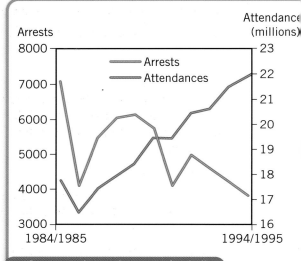

B Arrests and attendances at football league matches, 1984–1995

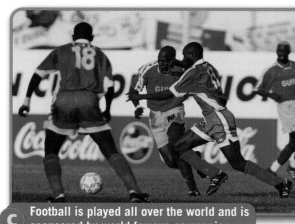

C Football is played all over the world and is sponsored by world famous companies

Merchandising – most clubs have a shop which sells football kits, scarves and other merchandise.

Sale of players – clubs also sell players to make money. Clubs in Divisions Two and Three may have to sell their better players to bigger clubs in order to raise funds to pay the wages of the club's other players and staff.

Recent changes in the football industry

There have been many developments in recent years:

- increased safety requirements
- the creation of the Premier League in 1992–1993
- increased media coverage from BSkyB
- the development of football as an industry, with some clubs now companies on the Stock Exchange
- huge increases in players' salaries and transfer fees
- redevelopment and relocation of football grounds.

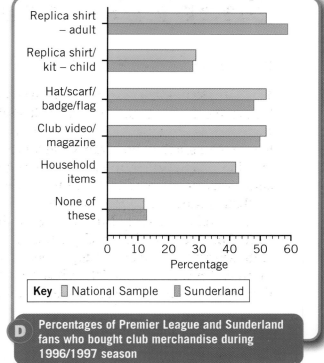

D Percentages of Premier League and Sunderland fans who bought club merchandise during 1996/1997 season

Activities

1 Study photograph **C**. How many different sorts of sponsorship can you see? Make a short list of ways in which sponsorship helps:
- the club
- the sponsor.

2 **a** Graph **A** is a *line graph*. Discuss with a partner what it tells you about football attendances.
b Use the help box to help you write a short summary of your findings. (123)

3 Study graph **B**. With a partner, discuss these two questions.
a What has happened to the number of arrests?
b Can this help explain the change in attendances? (123)

4 Graph **D** is a bar graph with lots of information showing what club merchandise different fans bought in one season. Write down three different facts that these graphs show. Include figures from the graphs to prove your statements. (123)

5 Which graph do you think shows the information best? Which is easiest to use? Give reasons for your answer. (123)

Research activity

6 Investigate the pattern of support for football in your class. You could focus on:
- which teams students support
- how often students watch football on TV, or attend matches
- what merchandising students have, and what they think about it.

Show your results using the best sorts of graphs for the data you have collected. Then make your conclusions. (123)

help!

Geographers often use graphs to show data. Graphs help them to investigate patterns and changes in the world around us. When you use graphs to investigate, try to:
- start with a sentence saying what the graph is about
- look for general patterns and changes (describe)
- include figures and examples
- if possible, think of some reasons for what you've found out (explain).

Where are football grounds located?

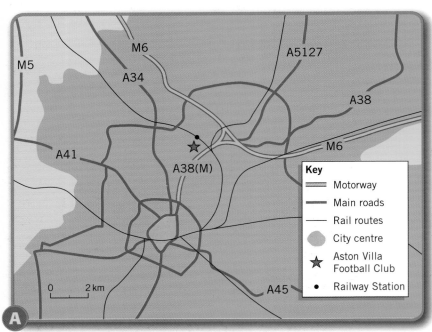

A — Map showing motorways, main roads, rail routes, city centre, Aston Villa Football Club and railway stations around Birmingham.

Key
- Motorway
- Main roads
- Rail routes
- City centre
- Aston Villa Football Club
- Railway Station

M6, A5127, M5, A34, A38, A41, A38(M), M6, A45

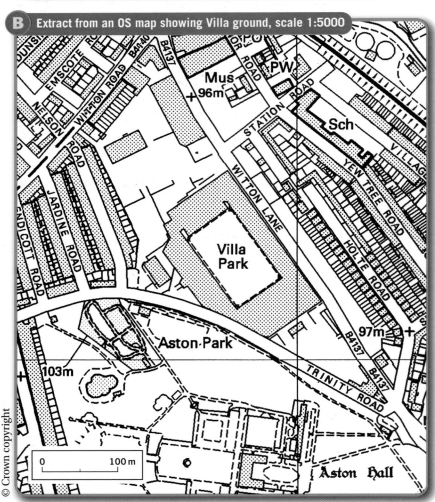

B Extract from an OS map showing Villa ground, scale 1:5000

© Crown copyright

Change at Aston Villa

Aston Villa Football Club started in 1874 as an amateur church team. The club grew and prospered and in 1897 they won the league and cup double. In the same year they moved to a new ground at Villa Park, **located** on parkland close to the northern edge of Birmingham. Working-class housing and industry quickly surrounded the ground. Map **A** shows that Aston Villa is now far from the edge of the city, because Birmingham has been built up so much. The club has plans to expand its ground but this has led to conflict with the local community.

The people of Aston

Twenty thousand people live in the area, 49 per cent of them young people under 24. The local community comes from many backgrounds, including 51 per cent Asian, 31 per cent white, and 14 per cent black people. Unemployment in the area is 23 per cent, compared with 10 per cent for Birmingham as a whole.

The place

Aston is typical of an inner city area built in Victorian times. Most of the housing is terraced. People with cars have to park them on the street. The main area of public open space is Aston Park, in the grounds of historic Aston Hall. There are shops along Witton Lane, large areas of industrial land and some car parks.

The impact of Villa Park

About three-quarters of Villa fans live within 45 minutes' travel time of Aston, and most people travel to the ground by car. Football matches at Villa Park cause a number of problems on match days. These include:

- increased traffic congestion
- on-street parking by football fans
- litter, noise and pollution
- antisocial behaviour
- disruption to people's daily routines.

Aston Villa's plans

The capacity of the Aston Villa ground is just under 40 000. The average attendance was 32 000 people per match in the 1999–2000 season. The directors of the club want to develop the ground so that it can seat 50 000 supporters. In order to expand, the club needs planning permission from the city council. The plans include:

- extending the North Stand and Trinity Road Stand
- redeveloping the Holte Hotel Public House into a 140-bed hotel
- closing or moving Trinity Road
- moving the Aston Play centre
- the loss of a playground, land and trees from the Park.

Aston Villa already employs 200 staff, with many more on match days. The new developments will create more jobs for local people.

C Aerial photo of Villa Park and its surroundings

Activities

1 Study the maps and aerial photo.

a Draw a sketch map of photo **C** to show the area around the football ground.

b Shade and label these land uses:
- Aston Villa's stadium
- Terraced housing
- Car parks
- Aston Park
- Industry
- Roads for parking (within 400 m of the ground).

c Now add these labels in the correct place on your map. They show the proposed changes, so use a different colour.
- New Trinity Road Stand
- Trinity Road blocked here
- New North Stand
- Holte Hotel redeveloped

2 Here are some groups of people in the local community:
- shopkeepers on Witton Lane
- residents of Jardine Road
- Aston Villa supporters
- young unemployed people
- parents with small children
- older residents.

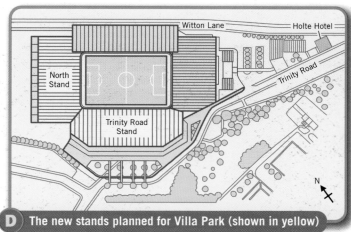

D The new stands planned for Villa Park (shown in yellow)

a Decide who will **gain** from the plans to extend the ground, and who will **lose**. Use a winners and losers grid, like the one below, to help you.

Winners	Losers
People: **shopkeepers on Witton Lane** Reason:	People: Reason:

b Discuss your answers with a partner. Why is it difficult to decide what a group of people might think?

DOES BIRMINGHAM CITY COUNCIL UNDERSTAND THAT THERE IS NO ROOM FOR VILLA PARK TO EXPAND?

Have the residents of Aston proved their point or not?

On 6 September 1998 more than 2000 people peacefully formed a human chain around the ground to protest against the expansion of the club.

They were protesting that their streets had been taken over by fans and their cars. They had been polluted by car fumes and rubbish had been thrown into their gardens. They had been imprisoned in their homes. Now they were expected to give up Trinity Road, which links the community and their park – the only recreation ground in the area. In return they would be expected to take all the abuse of fans coming into the area and stay quietly locked in their homes.

Aston Villa FC claimed it had been here for over 100 years and certainly before the current residents. This is not fair and the residents of Aston are getting angry. Now they want action to oppose the expansion and also to alleviate the problems being experienced now with the club.

Aston Neighbourhood Forum

Aston Federation of Churches and Mosques

E Development compass rose

Natural:
these are changes to the environment

Who decides:
the people who make decisions about the changes

Economic:
these are changes involving money

Social:
these are changes to people and the way they live

F The Villa Ground brings some benefits to the local community

Activities

1 A new development brings changes. The development compass rose helps you to look at these changes.

a In pairs, make a copy of the compass rose in **E** in the middle of a large piece of paper.

b Use all the information on pages 108–110 to work out the changes which the plans for Villa Park would bring. Decide whether they are Natural, Economic, or Social, or show Who Decides. Label these onto your compass rose.

c Colour code your labels to show which you think are changes for the better and which changes for the worse.

2 Are there more good points (better) or bad points (worse) on your compass?

3 Should the expansion plans for Aston Villa go ahead? What do you think the local council should decide? Explain the reasons for your decision.

Case Study

Oxford United – a club on the move

Oxford United is another football club near the middle of a big city. In 1995 Oxford United announced that they were to leave their Manor Ground at Headington because the site was too small. In 1996 the club started to build a new stadium to seat 15 000 people on a larger site with ample parking and room for many more facilities.

What was wrong with the old Manor Ground Stadium?

⦿ **Size:** The old Manor Ground, shown on Map **A** and photo **B**, has a small pitch, a stadium capacity of less than 10 000 fans, few facilities and no room to park. With few supporters paying to watch matches or use facilities, the club was struggling to make money. New rules for football stadiums meant that the capacity would have to be cut to 5000 fans – not enough to keep the club in business.

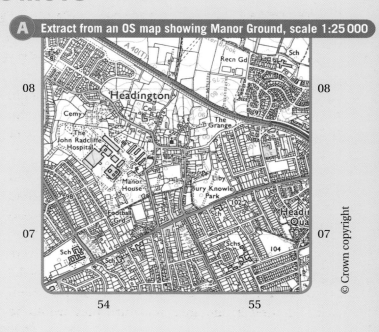

A Extract from an OS map showing Manor Ground, scale 1:25 000

© Crown copyright

B Manor Ground football ground, Oxford

⦿ **Location:** It is located in a high quality residential area with poor access and limited parking. Land is very expensive to buy here. The main entrance to the ground is from the busy A40 road. This is congested with shoppers and tourists on Saturdays. The Manor Ground is also close to Oxford's main hospital. Parking and road congestion on match days make it difficult for ambulances to reach casualties in the local area or to get to the hospital itself.

⦿ **Use:** The ground was only being used about 25 days each year – not enough to make a profit.

Why is it a good location?

◉ **Local opinion:** One survey of local people showed that people did not want the club to move. Residents thought that the club brought more advantages than disadvantages. Although some people mentioned the problems on match days of congestion, noise and graffiti, over 70% thought that the club brought benefits to the area. These included employment for players, caterers, coaches, groundsmen, physiotherapists and electricians. Football does not just employ footballers!

◉ **Local services:** The old Manor Ground has few facilities, so fans spent money in the local shops and pubs, bringing money and jobs to the neighbourhood.

C Extract from an OS map showing the Minchery Farm site, scale 1:25 000

The new stadium at Minchery Farm

With all these considerations in mind, the club decided to develop a new stadium. It would have all the facilities that the club needed, and the site would include a hotel, conference centre, multiplex cinema, banqueting centre, fitness centre, bowling alley, and an all-weather pitch. These would be used throughout the year, not just on match-days. The site will have parking spaces for 2000 cars and 15 coaches.

The new site has a number of advantages over the Headington site.

◉ There is room for a bigger stadium and plenty of parking.

◉ There are no other facilities nearby, so fans will spend more money in the stadium.

◉ There is plenty of room to develop new facilities although land is still quite expensive.

◉ It is quite close to the Blackbird Leys and Littlemore areas of Oxford, where workers live.

Activities

❶ Find the site of the Manor Ground on OS map **A** and Minchery Farm on Map **C**. Copy and complete the table below, comparing the two sites.

Similarities	Differences
1 Both are in the city of Oxford	1
2 Both are near to…	2
3	3

D Minchery Farm site, Oxford

Activities

2 a Look at the information about the Manor Ground, along with OS map **A** and photo **B**. Copy and complete this site survey for the Manor Ground by circling one number in each row

Lack of space	1 2 3 4 5 6 7	Plenty of space
No room to expand	1 2 3 4 5 6 7	Room to expand
Limited parking	1 2 3 4 5 6 7	Unlimited parking
Poor road access	1 2 3 4 5 6 7	Good road access
Expensive land	1 2 3 4 5 6 7	Cheap land
Few facilities in the ground	1 2 3 4 5 6 7	Many facilities in the ground
Few local facilities	1 2 3 4 5 6 7	Lots of local facilities
Expensive land	1 2 3 4 5 6 7	Cheap land
Few extra jobs created	1 2 3 4 5 6 7	Lots of extra jobs created

b Now look at the information about the new site at Minchery Farm, including Map **C** and photo **D**. Use another colour to circle the scores for the new site.

c Join up the scores for the Manor Ground with one colour, and the Minchery Farm scores with another colour.

3 Use your site survey to compare the two sites.

a Is there any way that the old site was better? If so, explain how.

b Is the Minchery Farm site perfect? Can you find any disadvantages for the football fans themselves?

4 Imagine that you are a resident of Headington (on Map **A**). You are fed up with the problems caused by people on match days. Write a letter to your local newspaper. Describe the problems and suggest what could be done about them. You can use the letter outline on the right to help you.

5 Now imagine that you are a local shopkeeper or pub owner in Headington. Your business benefits from the football supporters and you want to reply to the letter that you have just read. Here are some ideas to help you, but make your letter persuasive by adding facts and ideas of your own:

> I agree that … but I would like to point out that … only 25 days a year … 90 minutes …
>
> Although I accept that … 70% of local people say …
>
> I employ …

> 15 Beech Drive
> Headington
> Oxford
>
> Dear Editor
>
> I have lived in the Headington area for over twenty years, and I am writing about the problems that we suffer every time there is a match at the Manor Ground.
>
> Headington is a lovely place to live and it is a nice friendly neighbourhood, but every time there is a match…
>
> Most football supporters are… but…
>
> On one occasion last season…
>
> I think that, in future, the council should…
>
> I also believe that the football club should…

help!

Good geographers:

- ☺ think carefully about their own point of view
- ☺ present evidence carefully to support it
- ☺ include different types of information, such as sketch maps or labelled photographs
- ☺ remember that other people may have different views.

The World Cup

For football fans the FIFA World Cup is the greatest competition in the world. The first World Cup was held in 1930, and it has been held every four years since then, except during World War II. The winners of each football World Cup are shown in **A**.

France won the 1998 World Cup when they beat Brazil 3–0. The quarter-finalist countries are shown in **B**, with the level of economic wealth for each one. The average GDP per person for all the people in the world is $3610 per person.

1930	Uruguay	1970	Brazil
1934	Italy	1974	West Germany
1938	Italy	1978	Argentina
1950	Uruguay	1982	Italy
1954	West Germany	1986	Argentina
1958	Brazil	1990	West Germany
1962	Brazil	1994	Brazil
1966	England	1998	France

A World Cup winners

Quarter-finalist	GDP (US $)	Quarter-finalist	GDP (US $)
France	18 554	Germany	21 260
Brazil	2107	Italy	15 548
Croatia	4520	Denmark	23 690
Argentina	4021	Netherlands	18 369

B Quarter-finalists in the 1998 FIFA World Cup

Activities

1 On an outline map of the world, plot all the countries that have won the World Cup. Use a symbol to show how many times each country has won the trophy.

2 Compare your map with map **C**. Describe the distribution of 'World Cup winners'. Use these words to help you:
- Northern/Southern hemisphere
- MEDCs/LEDCs
- Europe/Africa/Asia/South America/North America.

3 Table **B** shows the quarter-finalists in 1998. How rich are the best football nations? The World average GDP per person is $3610, so how do these countries compare?

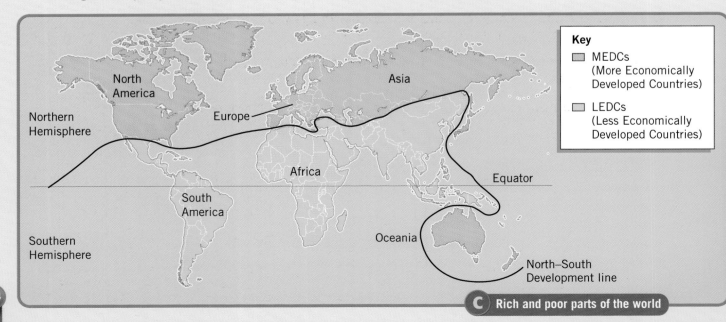

C Rich and poor parts of the world

Review and reflect

Key enquiry questions	Page numbers	Case studies or examples	What I learned about or did
Who takes part in or watches sport?	101		Planning an enquiry
Where are Premiership clubs located? What are their links with other parts of the world?	102–103		Plot distribution on a map
How do people get to football matches?	104–105		Planning routes
How is the football industry changing?	106–107		Finding information from graphs
Where are football grounds located?	108–113	Aston, Birmingham Oxford	The impact of football grounds on an area
How do people make decisions about changes?	108–113	Aston, Birmingham Oxford	Writing to persuade people
Which are the world's most successful footballing nations?	114		Describing and explaining patterns

Activities

1. Make a large copy of the table above. For each enquiry question, look back at your work for this unit and write the examples or places you have studied in the 'Case studies' column. One has already been done to help you.

2. The fourth column shows at least one thing you should have learned about or done for each enquiry question. For each one, check your work to see where you actually did this. Then add at least one more thing you learned.

3. Write down the three most interesting or important things you have learned about the world of sport. Explain why you chose them.

4. Write down two or three things you did or learned that might be useful in other subject areas.

5. Finally, write down which activities you found most difficult. Choose one or two targets you need to improve on in your next geography unit.

Glossary

Active volcano   A volcano that has erupted recently and is likely to erupt again.

Active zone   An area where two tectonic plates meet. Earthquakes and volcanoes occur in active zones.

Aid   Help that is given by one country to another, either after an emergency such as an earthquake or to help to improve living standards.

Annotated   An annotated sketch has labels that describe or explain the features that it shows.

Annual population growth rate   The difference between the birth rate and the death rate for a country. It shows whether the population is getting larger or smaller.

Anticyclone   A high-pressure weather system that brings settled weather, hot in summer, cold in winter.

Atlas   A book of maps that show different physical and human features of the world.

Birth rate   The number of babies born to every 1000 people in a country each year.

Capacity   The amount or number that something will hold.

Central Business District (CBD)   The area of a city where there are many shops and offices.

Climate   The average weather conditions of a place or region measured over many years.

Condense   Change from a gas into a liquid.

Confluence   The place where two or more streams or rivers join.

Core   Very hot rocks in the centre of the Earth.

Crater   A wide hole in the ground. The crater of a volcano is the hollow at the top of its opening.

Crust   The thin outer layer of the Earth.

Cyclone   A huge tropical storm, like a hurricane, with heavy rain and very strong winds.

Death rate   The number of people who die for every 1000 people in a country each year.

Depression   A low-pressure weather system that brings changeable weather, often rain, cloud and wind.

Destination   The place that someone is travelling to.

Development aid   Aid that is given to help a country to improve its living standards so that it can progress.

Diet   The usual food that people eat.

Dormant volcano   A volcano that is not active now but may erupt again.

Drainage basin   The area of land drained by a river.

Earthquake   Shaking and vibration of the ground caused by movements of the Earth's crust.

Economic asset   Something or somebody that makes money for a family or a country.

Economic burden   Something or somebody that costs a family or a country money.

Emergency relief aid   Aid that is given to help solve the problems caused by a disaster such as an earthquake or flooding.

Emigration   When people move out of a country to settle in another country.

Enquiry   An investigation to find out about people and places.

Epicentre   The point on the ground above the focus of an earthquake where the vibration is greatest.

Equator   An imaginary line round the middle of the Earth which represents the $00°$ line of latitude.

Eruption   When a volcano erupts, magma from inside the Earth escapes to the surface.

Evacuate   Take people from a place that is dangerous to a safer place.

Evaluation   Looking at something to see how well done or useful it is by looking at its strengths and weaknesses.

Evaporate   Change from a liquid into a gas.

Extinct volcano   A volcano that is unlikely to erupt again in the future.

Factor   One of the reasons for something.

Favela   Brazilian word for shanty town.

Focus   The focus of an earthquake is the point under the ground that the shock waves travel out from.

Front   A boundary or line between warm and cold air.

Geothermal energy   Heat energy from the Earth that can be used to generate electricity.

Global warming   The slow increase in world temperatures due to pollution in the atmosphere.

Groundwater   The water that flows beneath the ground surface.

Hypothesis   A theory about something that can be tested by an enquiry.

Immigration   The movement of people into a country.

Impermeable   A surface that does not allow liquid to pass through it.

Infant mortality rate   The number of babies who die before they reach their first birthday for every 1000 babies born.

Infiltrate   When a liquid sinks in through a permeable surface.

Informal work   Work which does not have a regular wage, and where the worker does not pay taxes.

In-migration   The movement of people into a place.

Inoculate   To protect someone from a disease by giving them a pill or injection containing a minute amount of the organism that causes it.

Irrigate   To transport water to an area where there is a shortage, usually for growing crops.

Labour   The workforce of a country or place.

Lahar   A mud-flow made of a mixture of volcanic ash and water.

Lava   Liquid rock that flows down the sides of a volcano.

Less Economically Developed Country (LEDC)   A country with a poor economy where many people live in rural areas.

Life expectancy   The average number of years that a person might expect to live. This varies from country to country, depending on diet, health care, etc.

Linear   A pattern that forms in a straight line.

Lines of latitude   Imaginary lines drawn around the Earth from east to west parallel to the Equator.

Lines of longitude   Imaginary lines drawn around the Earth from north to south and going through both Poles.

Location   The position of a place or other feature.

Location map   A map that shows where a place is in relation to other places and features.

Magma   Molten rock from beneath the surface of the Earth that escapes to the surface when a volcano erupts. It appears as liquid lava, volcanic bombs, ash, dust, steam and gases.

Magnitude   How large, strong or important something is.

Mantle   The middle layer of the Earth, made of hot, molten rock, between the crust and the core.

Migration   When people move from one place or country to another for a short time.

Minutes   Latitude and longitude are measured in degrees and minutes. There are 60 minutes in a degree.

More Economically Developed Country (MEDC)   A country with a wealthy economy where a high percentage of people live in urban areas.

Multinational   Multinational companies do business all over the world.

North–South Development Line   An imaginary line that separates the richer countries (MEDCs) of the north and Oceania from the poorer countries (LEDCs) of South America, Asia and Africa.

Official aid   Aid that is given by a government and paid for by its taxpayers.

Out-migration   When people move out of a place.

Perception   Viewpoint; somebody's opinion.

Permanent settlement   A place where people live throughout the year, such as a housing estate.

Permeable   A surface that allows liquid to pass through it.

Population density   The number of people per area of land. This is **high** when many people live in a place, or **low** where only a few people live.

Population pyramid   A type of bar chart that shows the population structure of a country. Because the number of babies goes at the bottom of the chart and the number of very old people at the top, the chart often looks like a pyramid.

Population structure   The age groups that make up the population of a country.

Precipitation   Water falling from the air to Earth as rain, hail, sleet or snow.

Prediction   Estimating what is going to happen in the future.

Primary data   Information that you find out for yourself by looking, counting or asking people questions.

Prime Meridian   The line 0 °of longitude that passes through Greenwich, near London.

Process of thinking   The learning process can be broken into four stages: cueing, acting, monitoring and verifying.

Relief   The shape of an area of land – whether it is flat, hilly or mountainous.

Richter Scale   The strength of an earthquake can be described using the Richter Scale. Each point on the scale is ten times bigger than the one below it. An earthquake measuring 7 on the Richter Scale is ten times stronger than one measuring 6.

Sanitation   Keeping places clean and hygienic, usually by a sewage system and a supply of clean water.

Satellite image   A photograph of part of the Earth's surface taken from a satellite in space.

Secondary data Information that you get from maps, books, CD-ROMs or the Internet.

Seismograph An instrument that measures the shaking of the ground to give the strength of an earthquake. It records the vibrations on a graph called a seismogram.

Self-build housing Houses built by the people who are going to live in them, for example in shanty towns.

Settlement A place where people live. It may be just a few homes or a large city.

Shanty town A squatter settlement, often on the outskirts of a city, built by people on land that does not belong to them.

Shock waves Shock waves travel out from the focus of an earthquake into the surrounding area, making the ground vibrate.

Site The exact location of a settlement. This often includes the physical features of the place it is built on, such as whether it is by a river.

Situation A general picture of where a place is. A settlement's situation can be described by looking at an atlas. It often includes physical features of the place it is built on, such as whether it is by a river.

Sparsely populated An area with a low population density, i.e. few people live there.

Stable population A population that is not getting larger or smaller because the death rate and the birth rate are the same.

Surface run-off The flow of water over the ground, including rivers and streams.

Symbol A sign used to represent something, such as a symbol on a map. A map has a key to show what each symbol means.

Synoptic chart A map that shows the areas of high and low pressure in a region at a particular time.

Tectonic plates The Earth's crust is made up of huge slabs called tectonic plates.

Temperate A climate, like that of the British Isles, that is neither very hot nor very cold is temperate.

Temporary settlement A place where people live for a short time, such as a nomad encampment or an oil rig.

Transnational A transnational company does business all over the world.

Transpire Leafy plants take water in through their roots and transpire it into the air as water vapour through pores in their leaves.

Tributary A river that flows into a larger river.

UNICEF United Nations Children's Fund.

Vegetation The plants in an area.

Venn diagram A diagram used to show the relationships within a set of items.

Vent The hole in the top of a volcano where lava escapes.

Volcanic bombs Lumps of lava that become hard as they fall from the sky during a volcanic eruption.

Volcano A hill or mountain through which molten rock from inside the Earth is able to escape to the surface.

Voluntary aid Aid that is given by people through charities such as the Red Cross.

Water cycle A continuous process in which water falls to Earth from the air as precipitation, evaporates and condenses to form clouds, and falls back to Earth again.

Weather The conditions of the atmosphere, such as the temperature, amount of rain or hours of sunshine.

Weather system An anticyclone or a depression.

Index